THE AWAKENED FEMININE

STORIES OF WOMEN AWAKENING TO WHO THEY TRULY ARE

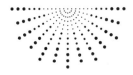

AMA PUBLISHING

CONTENTS

1. Ka Ki Lee   1
2. Adriana Monique Alvarez   11
3. Avalina Maline   18
4. Brooklin Rayne   27
5. Ellen Quach   38
6. Emily Ghosh Harris   49
7. Katya Barry   58
8. Linh Whyatt   69
9. Olivia Bangert   80
10. Safeera Kholvadia   92
11. Sarah Ashley Wheeler   105
12. Wendy Corner   111
13. Allie Xu   121
14. Cathleena Hailley   129
15. Celeste Palmer   138
16. Isabel Regina Esmann   147
17. Kathleen Quigley   158
18. Kimberley Jones   167
19. Leigh Elliott-Davies   176
20. Nadine Parkinson   187
21. Nicolette Wijers   196
22. Teena Ryan   206

About AMA Publishing   217

KA KI LEE

EVER EVOLVING

The awakened feminine is ever-evolving.

*Y*ou see, two and a half years ago, I had never even heard of the term "The Awakened Feminine," and even if I had heard it before, I would have had no clue what it even meant. Fast forward to today, two and a half years later, I now have such a deep appreciation and understanding of what "The Awakened Feminine" means to me right now and what it means to the women around me.

That is why it is my deepest desire to share with you where The Awakened Feminine came from and how it has awakened me since it came into my life.

One morning, yes, two and a half years ago, I was listening to an activation created by my mentor Regan Hillyer. As I was integrating after the activation, I heard a big loud voice say to me...

"START A PODCAST."

At that time in my life, a podcast was not on my list of things to do—it was not even on the list of things that'd be nice to do in the future because at that time I was trying so hard to get my online coaching business up and running amid a global pandemic. I was so busy working with my beautiful coach Emily Ghosh Harris as well as doing an online program that supposedly would help me set up a business (it didn't, but I'll save that story for another time) whilst my husband was working away, and my youngest daughter who is allergic to sleeping had just turned one.

I remember thinking to myself, "I don't even have time to scratch my bum, let alone start a podcast" but then I don't usually have a big loud voice telling me what to do either, so I said, "Okay. If I start a podcast, what do I do?"

In an instant, I received the name of the podcast, the premise of the podcast, the questions, and a list of names. I was in a daze. How could I have received all that information…instantly?

I knew there and then it was something that I had to do, and when I had my coaching session with Emily that evening, she agreed that starting a podcast was something I had to do.

One month after hearing that big loud voice, the first episode of my podcast was live for the world to hear.

I am still in awe of how quickly everything happened.

Guess what the name of my podcast is?

You got it.

The Awakened Feminine.

A place for women to share their love and wisdom.

Back then I had no idea what it even meant. All I knew was I had to keep the name because it was given to me, and it satisfied my desire to help women change their lives for the better.

So began my awakened feminine journey.

In the beginning, I didn't have a definition of the awakened feminine because I had no idea what it meant. The phrase felt foreign, even though I could tell you what I thought awakened and feminine meant. But those two words together? I was clueless. It makes me cringe a little sharing this with you but that was the mid-2020 version of me.

What is your definition of an awakened feminine?

It took me twenty-five episodes or three months later before I dared to ask my guests that question, and when I did, I started realising that I had so much to learn about the awakened feminine.

It awakened this curiosity within me. I felt like I was that child in the toy store that wanted to explore everything there is in the store, well, everything there was about the awakened feminine.

As each guest shared their definition of an awakened feminine, I was in awe of how unique yet similar their answers were. It was like there was an invisible thread linking all these women together, yet most of them did not know each other.

It was also three months after I launched my podcast that guests started to pitch to me to come on my podcast. I was so excited the first time I received a pitch email. It was as if the Universe was giving me a wink to assure me that I was heading in the right direction. The best thing is that every guest that pitched to me was like a gift from the Universe—they imparted their wisdom to me and my audience at the exact time I needed to receive their wisdom. They became messengers and teachers to me without knowing it, and the most fascinating thing was that I did not know it until later down the track as I reflected on all that came to be.

A couple of months after my podcast had her first anniversary, I met this amazing woman called Monique Alvarez for episode seventy. When I interviewed her, we went deep, we went to the most painful time of her life. I didn't expect to go there, but we did, and it was beautiful. My interview style had changed dramatically by then so instead of following a very structured question-and-answer style interview series, I am guided by my intuition and guides and sometimes I don't know where the conversation will go but what I know is that it always leads us to the most beautiful place, in the most beautiful way and what my guests share is exactly what they needed to share at that moment because our audience is waiting for that message, that inspiration, that wisdom.

The morning after our podcast interview, Monique emailed me and told me she was buzzing after our conversation and invited me to be part of her multi-author book. I remember reading the email, my whole-body tingling with excitement especially after seeing the title of the book: *Uncensored. Untamed. Unleashed.* Wow! I knew I had to be in the book, so I threw out my rule book for decision-making as an emotional generator and said YES.

Now the funny thing is that for the whole of 2021, I had been getting nudges and guidance to start writing, and for the whole of 2021 I told myself and my guides that I was too busy to write. The Universe, however, did not let me escape; instead, it delivered me a multi-author book on a silver platter. I can hear the Universe having a giggle and saying "Ha-ha, you are writing now! There is no escaping what is meant for you."

After *Uncensored. Untamed. Unleashed.* I was invited to another multi-author book, *Prosperity Codes*. Within six months I had shared my story in two multi-author books, and I was on a high from all the gifts I received from writing and sharing my story. It reignited my love for writing and then I started receiving guidance to write children's books, but the Universe had planned something else for me to do first and that was to lead my own multi-author book.

You see, after *Uncensored. Untamed. Unleashed.*, my husband planted the seed. He loved the multi-author book concept and thought it was great. He said to me, "You've got a podcast and all your guests want to share their story and this is another way for them to share their story!" I remember telling him, yes that is a great idea, but I don't know how and just parked the idea in our business ideas notebook.

Six months after the conversation with my husband, I ended up having a chat with Monique about publishing children's books, which led to the creation of the book that you are reading right now. What happened was when I was driving home on the day of our appointment, a book title came through—The Awakened Feminine: Stories of Women Awakening to Who They Truly Are. I remembered thinking, "That's strange," and letting it go. However, when I was talking to Monique about publishing children's books, I kept getting nudges to ask her about multi-author books, and when I told her the book title that came through, I got full body tingles as she said "Yes, we need that book." And so, the book was born.

The book cover is a phoenix because when I tuned into the book for the first time, I kept seeing a phoenix rising and lots of purples and blues. Every time after that whenever I tune into the book, I hear the phoenix calling and I see her spread her fiery wings behind me because I am the phoenix and so are all the women in this book.

The phoenix is strength and power because it comes back stronger each time it is reborn.

The moment I said yes to this book was the moment I unknowingly said yes to another period of tremendous growth and awakening. I remember a conversation I had with my soul sister Abigail who said to me, "The title of the book is the journey that you will take as you gather your soul family to co-create with you," and I can tell you now, that is exactly what happened.

The most profound lessons from my awakened feminine journey so far...

1. THE AWAKENED FEMININE IS EVER-EVOLVING

If you are living life, then you are ever-evolving. Most people are breathing but not living life because it is scary to live life fully, to explore, to listen to your guidance and actually go into the unknown. So, they just breathe and do the same things over and over expecting different outcomes or to feel different, but they don't, because they are doing the same things over and over again.

When you say yes to uncovering the hidden aspects of yourself, to stop judging yourself and accept the light and shadow, to forgive yourself for hurting yourself and others, to love yourself unconditionally and to live your truth without worrying about what others think then you are truly living. And no, you do not have to check all the boxes at once, all you have to do is start and everything will unfold.

2. DO THINGS YOUR OWN WAY

The winning formula to make a million dollars is different for everyone. Yes, there will be similarities and maybe some things will be the same but for the most part, you will find your own formula. So, if something doesn't feel good for you, stop doing it! The worst thing is to push yourself to do something you detest because your energy is going to be off, which means it won't work.

This has been true for me too many times. I'll invest thousands of dollars in a program only to find that the teachings are totally misaligned with my way of being, but I push because some coaches tell you that you are making excuses, or that you don't want it bad enough, or you need to push through or some other reason why you need to listen and follow their formula to the t or you'll FAIL.

I believed them at the beginning but now I know myself and how I operate. Pushing does not work for me. Hard work doesn't work for me. It is when I allow things to happen that it all comes together. There is still action to be taken but eighty percent of it is inner work and the rest the outer work.

I can assure you, if you trust yourself, you'll find your own formula.

3. YOU DON'T EVER HAVE TO DO ANYTHING ALONE

Before I entered the multi-author book world, I didn't know you didn't have to do anything alone. When I reflected on my life and business, I realised I also did everything on my own because I didn't want to burden others when I was the helpful one that saved the day.

How my world has changed in the last year!

This year opened my eyes to true collaboration through love and service and not I'll help you only if I have something to gain from it. I didn't know that existed. I didn't know that is the new way to do business and actually, to do life.

I remember being on a Zoom call with Monique and the question was "Why haven't you asked for help?" I raised my hand and gave my answer, which was "Why would anyone want to help me, and I don't want to burden other people." To which she responded, "If someone you know asked for help, I know you will be the first one to put your hand up and help because that's just who you are and that is why people want to help you because like attracts like."

Mic drop moment right there.

I was blown away because I had never thought about it that way.

I'm very good at going out of my way to help people but I never thought people would do that for me.

Isn't that crazy?

So from that day on, I learned that I never have to do anything alone again whether it's in life or business. Yes I am still learning to ask for help because sometimes the stories of unworthiness do come back, but I can tell you once you let those stories go, the people and opportunities that come your way will blow your mind.

4. EVERYTHING HAPPENS IN DIVINE TIMING

This one has been the most challenging for me. I am someone who wanted things done not yesterday, but last year. I am not patient, and I like everything to happen in my timeline.

This book is the perfect example.

The Awakened Feminine was originally scheduled to be published at the end of October, and I thought that would be a no-brainer. Little did I know that I had things to learn, clear, heal and let go of before it'll all come together.

At the start, I did all the things that I didn't like to do, and it was affecting my energy and made it difficult to find my soul family. I knew I needed support and after tuning in and consulting my divine team, I started working with my mama bear coach Therese Skelly who reminded me of my magic and helped me heal, let go, and clear some deep, ingrained stories and ancestral traumas.

At the end of September, everything started falling into place quickly but the ship had sailed for an October launch. Around this time, I received the date 12 December, and then for weeks after that, January 2023. However, I had put it out there on social media that this book was going to be launched on 12 December so I started pushing and creating anxiety not just for myself but for my soul family too.

What happened was that unbeknownst to me, my ego had taken the driver's seat and didn't want to push the date back because that would make me look foolish, but I knew I had to pluck my ego out of the driver's seat and trust in divine timing.

What a relief for everyone when that happened.

Once again I was reminded that the timeline is never under my control and to always trust in divine timing.

5. TRUST AND SURRENDER

Like divine timing, this was and still is one that I struggle with. After reading my story, you might believe that I am someone who trusts and surrenders but I can tell you that I don't always allow myself to trust or surrender, and that is when things don't work so well and I get to take the scenic route.

Obviously, it's a lot easier to listen to the big loud voices than the soft whispers. Starting a podcast was easy because the guidance I received was loud and direct, and I received all the information I needed instantly. It's the soft whispers that I find hard to hear or choose not to hear.

However, what I know is this: even if you did not trust and things did not go well and you took the scenic route, it would still have been the most beautiful unfolding. There was obviously something that you had to learn and once you get back on track, everything will fall into place.

Having said yes to uncovering myself to discover more and more of who I am and stripping myself naked in public (metaphorically) by sharing my vulnerable stories requires a lot of trust, and I can tell you I have been on many scenic routes. Unfortunately, sometimes scenic routes are terrible when you are there and only hindsight will allow you to see the scenery but remember...

It was meant for you.

You are the person you are today because you trusted and surrendered (sometimes) and took the scenic routes other times.

It is all perfect.

So what is my current definition of an awakened feminine?

An awakened feminine is a woman who knows and lives her truth.

She no longer follows the rules because she makes her own rules. She knows what works for her and what doesn't, and she doesn't need anyone telling her what to do. She knows her value, her desires, her uniqueness. She is sovereign, she is powerful, yet she is kind. She is in touch with her emotions, she is not afraid to stand for what she believes in, and she is a creatrix. She dances in harmony with her divine masculine and feminine and at her very core, her essence is love.

That is my definition right now, and I know that as I continue my awakened feminine journey (because once you start, it never ends), my definition will evolve because the awakened feminine is ever-evolving.

I'll love to know…

What is YOUR definition of an awakened feminine?

ABOUT KAKI LEE

Ka Ki Lee is the founder and creator of The Abundant Goddess Academy and host of The Awakened Feminine podcast. Ka Ki teaches busy women how to create money on the US stock market in less than thirty minutes per week, regardless of market conditions. She is here to change the stock market landscape by bringing in intuition, feminine flow and a strategy and language that is easy to understand. Ka Ki became inspired to teach the strategy, mindset, and energy tools she used to replace her six-figure income as a hospital pharmacist manager because she knew first-hand how exhausting it was to exchange time for money, and this was a perfect way for busy women to create money effortlessly—in minimal time! Her podcast, The Awakened Feminine, is ranked in the top 10% globally, and features inspiring women (and a few good men) from around the world, sharing their journey and message to living a soul-led life. Ka Ki is also a two time #1 international best-selling author, an executive contributor for Brainz magazine, and has been featured in numerous podcasts. She currently lives in Perth, Western Australia, with her husband, Terry, and two young daughters.

Website: www.kakilee.com
Instagram: www.instagram.com/abundancewithkakilee
www.instagram.com/theawakenedfemininepodcast
Facebook: www.facebook.com/abundancewithkakilee
LinkedIn: www.linkedin.com/in/kakilee

2

ADRIANA MONIQUE ALVAREZ

*I*t was the middle of the night in the middle of winter when a Being transported me from my cozy bed to the top of a mesa. This Being that cannot be described did not have form like we have form. It was more than form, it was a knowing and a feeling.

The view from the top of that mesa was incredible. Colors are what I remember most. Vibrant colors in every direction. I felt safe and it felt familiar like I had been there before. I sat on the edge and my legs dangled off. From this place I could see my life from conception to death. Instead of a series of experiences and choices that seemingly have no rhyme or reason, I saw a tapestry. A tapestry that looked like it had been woven by someone with great experience. There was no chaos or misplaced threads, it was art.

What the Being shared with me was the message that would wake me from a deep slumber. While the message was strong, it had zero hints of judgement or shame. It was pure love. Not the kind of love that makes us feel good alone. Love that cannot see us being anything less than we chose to be.

The Being shared that each person who chooses to live on Earth selects a way to arrive and way to exit. We call these birth and death.

There is nothing wrong or right about any of the options, they are simply how we get here and how we leave. Once we get in this human body we make many things about these two problematic. We write novels about how some ways are better than others and we bring much pain on ourselves and others in this practice. The Being held me in deep love and gently said, you have done this to yourself. You have made the entrance that you chose a source of great pain. You have questioned it and blamed yourself for things you need not blame yourself or anyone else for. This practiced over the years has created holes in your being. You have good things running out of those holes and you know it. You know it and have tried to plug those holes with many things.

Your favorite has been achievement and success. You have found many ways to do it. You did it! You got there. The only problem is achievement and success, while good in many ways, beneficial to you and others, cannot plug those holes. When you had awareness about this you took the next step, you bought things for yourself and others to fill the void. That didn't work either. You improved yourself and that was lacking in hole filling as well. You gave back. You gave to many, many people. You tried so hard and yet the holes remained.

We could see that you had buried yourself in a hole that was becoming difficult to find your way out of. You convinced yourself that the real problem was you had not achieved enough. So you hyper focused on it. You did everything in your power to get better at what you do and you asked for guidance and support in your business. You amazed even yourself. You achieved more than you ever dreamed of. You succeeded at a level very few will in one lifetime. Instead of being in awe your eyes adjusted and instead of seeing what you had, you only could see what you didn't have or more accurately, what you could have if you kept at it.

You asked for support daily and one day you asked for assistance on fulfilling your soul's purpose. You thought you knew what you were asking for, but you didn't. A messenger was sent in the form of a baby. You thought it was like your previous two babies, but this soul was not to stay. It was to get your attention and help you course correct.

The messenger did get your attention.

Right then I heard my own voice in the air, like a video that was being played back.

"I was not willing to lose anything else. I had to keep the business going. I had to retain our clients. I had to keep my marriage and keep mothering my boys. And oh by the way, deal with my grief."

The Being looked at me and right then I got it. I never, not once, considered taking care of me at that time. I never thought I needed to address my healing and wholeness.

If it meant my business, marriage, and boys would be better, I did it.

But I didn't do anything for me.

I had it backwards. I still thought the most important thing was to keep my life, as it was on track. I thought retaining myself as I was, my life as it had been, was the point. It was not the point! I only could see it right now as I sat on the mesa.

My heart quivering asked, what is the point? Why am I here? Why did I come? I cannot remember. There are many wonderful things, projects, and people I could pour myself into. But I do not want to do that anymore. I want to remember.

A still, small voice answered:

"To give and receive love."

That was not the answer I was hoping for. It sounded a bit like a Hallmark card. No really, why am I here? What mark shall I leave? What shall I do? What do I want to be remembered for?

To give and receive love.

This was the answer. What does that mean exactly? I asked.

To give and receive love each day. Can you do that?

I simultaneously felt silly and challenged.

Of course I can give and receive love every day. I think I am already doing that. What else you got for me? I mean I am capable of more than that. Isn't there more important work for me to do?

What could be more important?

I stopped talking back and felt those words in my heart. To give and receive love each day. I might already be doing that, but what if that was the focus and the most important thing of all? What would change if I knew and understood that is the point of me being here? I could feel my insides change. My cells danced. I tingled all over and the colors got even more vivid. My senses heightened. And in that moment I felt peace wash over me and take residence in my heart. While I was still seated on the mesa, it seemed as if I had moved to a different location because I saw the scene from a different perspective. I saw my life in a new way. Of course my approach would change.

Before the Being returned me to my body and bed, it said to me, there will be people who mean very much to you who will have to make peace with how you choose to go and that is their work.

As you focus on the reason you came here and you give and receive love each day, this peace you know right now will stay. The holes will fill, not from anything or anyone, but with the love that is flowing through you and to you.

This is who you really are and this is why you came into this body and this experience. Before you jumped into that body we sat here and you wrote the script. You selected teachers, guides and messengers. You chose it all and you signed off on it. You were completely dedicated and committed to it. And you told the circle around you to keep you on track, no matter what. When life shakes you up, when it feels painful or confusing, come back to this moment and know it's all pointing you back to yourself, to your reason for being here, and to your commitment to it. Remember the stories you create, the ones you write and refine and retell, make this either more enjoyable or more painful.

You are writing the script. You are always writing the script.

Your husband is the love of your life. Your boys are precious. Your parents. Your niece. The people around you who love you, they are the point. The love that flows between you. Highlight it and bask in it. There are other things you will do, Earth tasks like laundry and grocery shopping and there are ways you will create exchange with people so your life has things you enjoy experiencing. And I'll remind you of a little secret that you already know…

When love is where you live and your whole being is benefiting from the love that is flowing to you and through you, the Earth tasks, systems and exchanges will always be much easier and more enjoyable. Resources will never be difficult to access, retain or exchange when you keep the point your priority.

You are never alone. You are surrounded by support and your heart knows the way. Trust it all. That is peace. That is what makes you whole.

This is who you really are and how you can live the rest of your days and when you cross the bridge and your are walked home, you will never regret how you spent your energy if you do this. You will not need a particular achievement or success. You will not need to create a legacy. You will not need to gift the world anything in particular. You will not need to teach your boys something special. Your life will be your message, your legacy, and your gift. It will be all your boys will ever need. Every living being benefits when you remember the point of your life. Every living being. The planet herself. The entire cosmos. One life lived according to its purpose has a ripple beyond what you can comprehend right now. But one day we will return here and you will see it for yourself and you will know and you will be filled with gratitude and awe.

The Being that cannot be described transported me back to my body and back to my bed. I could feel my body taking its time. My eyes stayed closed for longer. I felt my soft cream blanket, I saw the curtains and light shining through. I saw Derek and I remembered everything from my time on the mesa.

It felt as though I had a new body and a new mind. I felt whole and at peace. When I am tempted to believe I need to focus on something that makes me sound more important or helps me achieve something admirable, I will remember the point.

To give and receive love each day.

I will wake up each day and ask, how shall it look today?

What a life this is! My life work is now to do this. When I get afraid and I feel like a fool I will remember that she is no fool who loves each moment, each person, and each experience. She is no fool who is at peace with herself and others. She is no fool who is alive and with the moment.

She is no fool who knows who she is and why she is here.

She is no fool who can live in love each day.

That is who I really am.

ABOUT
ADRIANA MONIQUE ALVAREZ

Adriana Monique Alvarez is the CEO and Founder of AMA Publishing. She is an unconventional visionary whose life and business was inspired by a decade of travel and volunteer work around the world. She is a USA Today best-selling author and a 19 time international bestselling author. She is an artist, photographer, and private chef for her husband Derek and two sons Sam and Grant. She is currently living in the middle of nowhere Colorado where she is renovating her grandparents home and learning how to homestead.

Website: *www.amapublishing.co*

3

AVALINA MALINE

*U*pon reflection on my youth, two aspects stand out. I chose not to listen to what was being taught to me in school. More specifically, I just wasn't interested. My disposition toward authorities was challenging—one could assume that I was a bit wild and quite determined to not be controlled. This of course got me in a wee bit of trouble here and there but ultimately led me onto a journey of self-discovery.

The other is that I've been consciously dreaming on a regular basis from a very young age. I remember going to sleep every night often very excited knowing that I was about to explore a completely different reality with an entirely different set of abilities. This seemed very normal to me, and I assumed most people had similar experiences in dreamtime. It wasn't until many years later when I came across a book on astral dynamics that I started to explore my history of lucid dreaming. I realized how much more there was to our reality and who I was. It sparked my awakening. I began experimenting and practicing projecting my astral body outside of my physical body from a waking state. I became very adept with this very quickly. The first out-of-body experience I had radically changed my entire belief system. Knowing and feeling that my essence was not the physical body was the most exciting and freeing shift that I could have imagined. All meaning in my life changed, and my priorities and desires shifted along with it. So many things fell away in my life very naturally with little effort. I could no longer stick to what I thought I wanted; I could only go with where my heart was leading me which not only made life much more easeful but also joyful.

I absorbed everything I could get my hands on related to spirituality and enlightenment. It was a constant awareness and dedication that never left me. The very first time I sat down to meditate, within a few minutes, I had a massive surge of energy run up through the center of my head, accompanied by the brightest flash of white light I had ever seen. It was as if this energy was just waiting for me to engage and give it the space it needed. This pulse of energy and light often became a reoccurring event upon deep relaxation of my mind.

Through a series of synchronicities, I was led to using sound as a medium, and it was through toning that my physical body moved into a higher vibration. Toning daily brought about the most powerful kundalini awakening that brought forth many mystical experiences. The first time I toned using a specific repetitive sequence, as if speaking to my body's cells in their language, I actually received a response. A series of audible sounds was playing inside my body as if responding to the language that initiated a cellular awakening. My entire body felt like a cosmic tuning fork. It was a strange phenomenon that my body could actually produce sound within me that continued to speak back to me with startling enthusiasm that lasted about fifteen minutes. With daily repetition of toning, I could feel the electromagnetic charge shifting in my body, which initiated a massive rapid detox that lasted for many weeks. I noticed my body began leading me more in what it wanted and didn't want. I no longer had any desire for many foods, especially dairy or meat, nor could I handle caffeine or sugar. It wasn't a mental choice. I actually no longer enjoyed them or had any desire for them so they just fell away. It wasn't for a few months that I realized "well, I guess I'm a vegetarian now." My intuition increased and my sleep patterns and energy levels changed.

The external reality of my life was completely changing along with my internal state of being. I no longer had an interest in participating in the lifestyle that had previously been my norm. The increase in awareness I had shifted my perspective of all of my relationships, with myself, others, and the world. I could no longer be in the career I was in, many friends vanished from my life, and I even moved to a different state. All of this was not actually challenging. You would think when every aspect of your life changes, it would be, but it was so natural and effortless. All these changes felt good, and I was following my inner knowing. There was no doubt; I just knew and it was non-negotiable.

The inspiration that came along with these experiences was so exciting that my whole outlook on life became lighter and I actually began to dream bigger of what was possible. Life had such a deeper meaning and purpose. The profundity that this is just one experience as a human and that my true nature is so much greater continued to expand as I uncovered more and more limiting beliefs I was holding on to. At the time of my awakening, most people were not awakened to the truth of who they were or why they were here, so they didn't quite understand what I was going through or could relate to my experiences, so it was more of a solitary path. Yet I was aware it would only be a matter of time before more of humanity awakened. My inner compass had become the foundation of every aspect of my life, and I didn't waver in my knowingness.

An interesting aside to this is I could see the threads throughout my life where I was tapping into this knowingness but for the most part, I had been going along with what was considered "normal." All this time I just hadn't been trusting myself. The guideposts were always there, left, right, and center. Stepping into deeper trust I thought would require courage. Yet the more I began to trust, the more I realized I didn't need courage. If I'm in complete full trust then there is no fear to arise so there's no need for courage or anything else. Replacing courage with trust allowed my mind to relax, and I was able to give myself space to enjoy whatever I was moving through.

The more this journey unfolded so did the felt sense of responsibility and self-work that came along with it. Accepting what life was showing me through circumstances, situations and events was the most challenging yet ultimately came to be the most rewarding. Could I surrender to what my current projected reality was showing me? Knowing that I am the creator of my reality and therefore revealing all to myself in order to return to the fullness of my true essence.

My ultimate test in surrendering came when I was told I had a second detached retina. I had one before in the other eye years earlier and had invasive surgery to correct it so I had been down this road before and was not keen on repeating it. I had to ask myself "what's the worst-case scenario here and can I be ok with it?" I allowed my mind to go down the rabbit hole of all things terrible in this situation: "I could potentially be blind in this eye and then develop a lazy eye," etc. I had to tell myself "okay this is happening" and bring myself into a complete space of neutrality knowing that any of these outcomes were possible. I had to trust that whatever happens is for my highest good, knowing that there's a gem on the other side of any challenge. So, if this is the path I'm creating to get there then I am going to let this reality show me no matter how the outcome unfolds. As soon as a dropped into this acceptance, there was no more drama around it anymore. I felt free from it. I let go of any expectation or attachment to the outcome. I began to relax, and while feeling no contraction in my body I allowed space for healing while believing that it was possible. I ended up not needing the surgery at all; my eye miraculously healed.

So being worried in the first place was the only thing that had actually caused me any suffering. I could have just trusted from the beginning that whatever happened would have been perfect for my evolution.

So as a creator being, why would I create challenging circumstances? I quickly began to see that the greater the challenge, the greater the opportunity for transformation. Whenever I stop trying to control and trying to get out of that which I don't like, there was an absolute flow that would happen almost like a dam erupting. It's the opposite of how we have been programmed to live. We've been programmed to fix, to change, to get out of, to be comfortable, and to be in control. When the way we are actually designed to be as multi-dimensional humans is in a complete and utter state of surrender, trust, openness and expansion. That's when the floodgates open—when we allow ourselves to be in that state even in those moments where it's not how we would like it to be. So it's having that faith that allows the magic to happen. When you have that faith, then the present moment becomes far more enjoyable and an easier one to maneuver through.

When I began to trust is when the shifting and letting go accelerated. Trusting in what resonated with me and in the voice of my Higher Self was actually more true than anything else I was believing or perceiving in the exterior world. Perhaps I was actually on to something in my pre-teen rebel days. My focus then became holding the understanding that every circumstance and occurrence was being created for me by me and that every experience is here to serve me if I choose to hold the broader perspective and see the opportunity that's in front of me. Choosing to see things this way took the pressure off and made walking through life so much more enjoyable. I could still hold on to joy even in the midst of uncertainty and undesirable situations.

My mind's job is to bring up ongoing thoughts to trigger the emotions that society and any conditioning have taught me to avoid. Each time this happened was another opportunity for me to see where I was holding on to beliefs that were not serving me. The more I allowed myself to understand, feel, and process my emotions, the more my mind would quiet down, which became the process for me to further understand and be at one with all of me.

The deepening of the spiritual journey didn't mean losing the feeling of my emotions. Instead, it meant gaining an understanding of their importance as part of the human and spiritual journey. My focus began to shift into no longer ignoring even the basic emotions. No more tendency to pull away from a 'negative' experience and their difficult inner emotions without understanding that this journey will eventually have you face it head-on.

I developed a constant dedication to holding the awareness that I was choosing in every moment the perspective of what life was showing me. It became apparent that the perspective I was choosing at any moment was directly related to the emotional state I was in. My emotional body was just the bridge from the mental body to the physical and I was the one actually choosing my emotional state. The perspective then was the key to allowing the experience of peace and Joy. Could I actually allow myself to be in a constant state of joy?

Why would I be happy and joyful sometimes and then not feel it at other times? It occurred to me how strange and unnatural this was; that I could allow my external reality to dictate how I felt. Seeing that I was not one to follow the rules from early on, why was I letting anything outside of me determine my state of being—clearly giving my power away and following the illusion that life is happening to me rather than owning it and honoring that it's actually all happening for me.

Experiencing any suffering of any kind is simply pointing to what needed to be addressed internally. If there is any emotional pain then it's a matter of shifting my perspective from the illusion that any feeling of centeredness, peace and love I had prior to whatever instigated this unwanted feeling was ever outside of me. Where did go? Why did I let it go? If I was to continue thinking that what I felt from any experience, labeled good or bad, was coming from that experience or because of that experience then all I'm doing is creating attachment, which just perpetuates more suffering.

I came to realize that emotional pain or suffering has nothing to do with love. There's no pain in love; there is no flip side to love. Any feeling of pain is simply because of the projected outward feeling of love being attributed to something or someone external. When the love that is felt was inside you all along. It was mine, to begin with, and has always been available to me. I just wouldn't allow myself to see it until "this or that" happened. When I was in agreement and content with my reality, I was allowing it to show me what was inside me, literally the mirror for me to see what was inside myself. When I realized that all the love I've ever felt at any point in my life was there inside me because it came from me, that I could feel it anytime, all the time, every moment and that it has always been there, I didn't need anything to feel it, that if I fully embracing that love then I would become Whole. Then there is no loss when change occurs because there is nothing to lose, I would already be Full of love and no one could take that away from me but myself. I began to let go and realized how I felt at any given time was never about anything else or event in my reality but simply how much I was allowing myself to love myself. When love is the guiding barometer, we become that frequency of love and lose the ability to judge, you see everything as innocent and you see the world that way. When you elevate your frequency to love or above you literally are making waves in the collective consciousness.

I found having compassion for myself for what I was feeling and being authentic in the moment exactly as I was giving myself the full-on experience of being all that I truly am right in the very moment no matter how uncomfortable, or triggered, or what the physical experience might be, to let myself relax into it and have it so I can do that deeper level healing, clearing, shifting, which then allowed me to have a more genuine experience of joy in the body.

It's easy to make the spiritual journey overcomplicated with so many different teachings and information available but sticking to the basics and keeping it simple can offer profound transformation. As long as I remained fully present as the observer and aware of what I was choosing every moment, everything would unfold in the best way my Higher Self intends. Paying attention to my self-talk, the lens of perception I was choosing, the actions I was or wasn't taking, listening to inner guidance and what my body was feeling and needed, all pointed to me taking response-ability—literally my ability to respond at any given moment either to the external or within myself. Not only did this take the pressure off me of "was I doing enough or I should be doing this," etc., but everything would just flow with such ease. I was allowing the simplicity of daily life to be my teacher. Lessons don't have to be huge or monumental, they can be small. Some of the greatest lessons can come from the seemingly insignificant. I began to notice and to never dismiss what was right in front of me. All the insight was there if I gave myself the opportunity to see and pay attention. We are not separate from our reality and everything around us. It is always reflecting back to us who we are choosing to be.

So what was the essential ingredient I needed in every moment? … more love. If I could distill the entire spiritual journey down to one thing, it all came down to love. The saying "love transmutes all" can never be undervalued. The simplicity of honoring and loving yourself can move mountains. We are all powerful beyond words and have the ability to direct our journey and evolution. So simply put: What are you going to choose today?

There were many times in the early part of my journey that I wished things had been different or the awakening process had unfolded in a more preferable way or faster, often judging myself or my experience, but I now have gratitude for the divine unfolding that I chose for myself knowing now that it couldn't have been more perfect. I continue this journey with gratitude and joy as I forever uncover more and more depth of evolution that's possible and my heart is filled with excitement for all the endless potential this human experience continues to unveil.

ABOUT AVALINA MALINE

Avalina Maline offers exceptional support for the awakening process by sharing her gifts as an intuitive channel, an awakened multi-dimensional consciousness, and through her inner-standing of quantum energy to accelerate and harmonize awakening, embodiment, and the transformation of consciousness. She received a B.A. in Business and French Literature from North Carolina State University and has a diverse background, from building homes to performing arts as a singer and musician. In 2010 she had a powerful Kundalini awakening, and recognized her sense of I Am shifted from her limited human perspective to her soul consciousness. She has since passionately continued her evolution and will meet your mind, heart, and soul through your multidimensional nature and unfolding stages of awakening, integration and self-realization.

To empower individuals to greater embody their divine Truth, Sacred Sovereignty and Higher Purpose, Avalina offers transmissions, courses, private sessions, and speaking engagements to support and facilitate the embodied awakening process.

> *Website:* www.CreatorEssence.com
> *Email:* avalinamaline@gmail.com
> *YouTube:* @avalinamaline
> *Facebook:* www.facebook.com/avalinamaline
> *Instagram:* www.instagram.com/avalinamaline

4
BROOKLIN RAYNE

~Ask and you shall receive.
~Surrender and doorways beyond your linear imagination open.
~Trust and all that you seek to experience will be created as your reality.
~Show up consistently and presently each day and the pathway to Self real-
ization quickens. ~Become the witnessing presence of your life and all will be
revealed.
~There is nothing to fear, but fear itself.
~To experience life through the lens of childlike curiosity and innocence is to
remember and embrace the true nature of our divine essence.

*A*ll of these streams of wisdom spoken throughout the ages, and often written off as cliche, are some of the foundational threads that best describe my spiritual journey thus far.

They are the wisdom keepers that I connect to each and every day as I navigate through the 3rd-dimensional seas of the unknown ~

I remember so clearly the summer day, now a decade ago, when I reached my surrender point. On paper and to all around me, my life seemed pretty perfect. I had three beautiful, healthy, happy children, and a successful and kind husband. I had reached the pinnacle of success, in my then over fifteen-year career, as a chef and concept creator. I was running marathons, eating healthy, and had a thriving social calendar. Seemingly perfect through the lens of the 3D observer.

However, on the inside, an internal storm had been brewing, and it could no longer be kept at bay. I had reached the pinnacle of my inner suffering on an emotional, mental, physical, and spiritual level. And I had exhausted all that I knew to assist me in creating change.

I remember crying and literally throwing my hands in the air that day, saying to Source, "Ok! I surrender! I surrender! What do I need to do to get myself to a place of inner peace? To release and let go of this internal prison?" Immediately I heard a voice say "It's time to meditate."

"What? Meditate? Whose voice was that? I don't know how to meditate!"

Further crying ensued. A proper bathing of sorts, in the programs of self-pity and victimhood that I had chosen to know and experience all too well in this lifetime.

After I felt complete in my expression of self-pity, I allowed the deep awareness and knowing that my pleas had been answered by the voice of Source. And although I didn't know anything about meditation that was exactly what I was going to do.

Part of the internal storm that I had masterfully created as my reality included an incessant amount of mind chatter. Seemingly endless streams of unworthiness, self-judgement, guilt, shame, fear of failure, perfection, and "not enough" programs played out on repeat in a 3D symphony within my ego mind. I had become an expert in embodying self-hatred programs.

That said the beginning journey of my meditation practice felt like a mountain seemingly impossible to climb. I set the timer for up to fifteen minutes every day, closing my eyes, breathing, and setting the intention to release all that no longer served me and to embody Divine peace in exchange.

When I first set out on this inner quest with meditation I would peek at the timer multiple times throughout the fifteen-minute practice. Hoping for the agony of trying to quiet the mind chatter would soon end.

And albeit the beginning of my journey of deeper surrender and release through meditation was challenging, I had a deep faith, trust, and surrender in the full knowing that this was the guiding light to inner peace and freedom. What I did not know was that I was on a super highway of spiritual expansion and my whole life was about to change in profound ways.

Within a few short months, I had a prolific experience take place during meditation. I set the timer for fifteen minutes and a few hours later I was coming out of a state of what I can only describe as pure Source connection.

A tremendous amount of light began to pour into my body. With my eyes closed all I could see was a piercingly bright gold, violet, and white light. I sensed a massive shift taking place within all my bodies and a deep and unwavering embodied knowing that we are Source.

It was in that experience that it became exponentially clear what I am here for. It was revealed that this inner itch and knowing that I had carried with me through my entire life was about to open up and blossom into its greatest expression; I AM here in the greatest service to all beings seen and unseen in accordance with the highest Source Creator Unity, Light, Love, Law and Order. To restore the Christos template and immaculate unified field of consciousness.

From that experience forward I was on a fast track to awakening. I was experiencing profound and plentiful synchronicities daily. The more I surrendered and followed my inner knowing and intuition center of the heart, the more the universe led me to the people and places that inspired my next steps of spiritual awakening and expansion of consciousness.

From meditation followed Sacred Breath. Leaps and bounds of inner alchemy and soul retrieval were taking place through these consistent daily practices. I was witnessing my entire reality and perception of reality change rapidly. Manifesting my intention of inner peace and freedom.

I was coming home into the greater embodied knowing that we

are eternal individuations of Source having an experience as human incarnates. And that we predetermined and co-created with Source our blueprints for this incarnation.

This knowing was a key catalyst and foundational truth, allowing me to embody more and more of my Higher Self. Participating as the witnessing presence. And dissolving more and more of my identification as the ego mind complex.

Through this massive metamorphism that was taking place, I was guided to complete my journey as a chef and to begin exploring ways to share with others the tools that I was acquiring and practicing daily.

As I am sure you can imagine the vast and rapid changes that were taking place within were incomprehensible to many in my life. I really did not have anyone in my family and friend groups that knew anything about awakening, spirituality, and ascension. I received a lot of criticism and judgement from others along the way.

I knew from the moment of my surrender, that summer day in 2013, that it was time to wake up and shed all the layers of duality, polarity, and distortion no matter what anyone outside of myself had to say or think about it.

Of course that doesn't mean I was not triggered by others' resistance to my path and their many attempts to prevent me from further expansion and growth. I absolutely was! And I am grateful for every single one of them.

They assisted me in seeing and knowing where I have subscribed to limiting beliefs and fear programs. Where I had chosen to give my freedom and sovereignty away to systems of limitation and separation. I began to realize more and more how all of the people in our reality can be catalysts for our journey to Self-realization if we allow them to be.

I began to get certified as a holistic health coach, trained in Sacred breath, color light therapy, and much more. All was flowing and shifting rapidly and the embodiment of peace and light was palpable. I continued to have an unquenchable inner thirst to seek as much knowledge about spirituality, awakening, and the return home into full Self-realization.

Soon into my certification process for health coaching, I sent out a clear declaration to the Universe that I was ready to serve through my newly created practice "Mindful eating. living. breathing." Within twenty-four hours of my declaration, the universe responded back. A mom of one of my boys' friends "unknowingly" reached out to me seeking guidance on assisting her son.

I was amazed and humbled by the Divine perfection of it all!

What made it even more incredible was that the night before she called me, in a dream state; I dreamt about a child who had a rash on his body. In the dream, I knew that I was being called to help him.

During our phone call, the mother described the autoimmune diagnosis that her son received and explained how he had a rash on his body. And thus the new chapter of my journey of service to all began. ~

About three years into this magical journey another layer of my path of service revealed itself. It was a mid-October day, and I woke up feeling a deep calling rising within me.

As I completed my morning routine of getting my three boys off to school, I found myself in communication with Source: "I know that I have many spiritual pots on the stove right now, but I am ready for my next big assignment. Immediately I heard a voice within say, "go to Barnes and Noble." I laughed, as I literally had a stack of newly purchased books of spiritual nature awaiting me on my nightstand. I allowed the message to take a seat in the back of my consciousness and continued on with my busy day.

Before I knew it, it was time for me to pick up the boys from school. As they got into the car my oldest son asked, "mom, can we go to Barnes and Noble?" My heart began to flutter in amazement. My children had never made this request before. In fact, they may have gone to Barnes and Noble only once before in their lives.

Once there, I immediately headed to the spiritual section. Standing before all of the books, the realization that I was a spiritual book hoarder became clear! I had so many of the books that were displayed before me.

Stepping back slightly, I asked Source, "Ok, why am I here?" And just as I was asking that a book caught my eye: *St. Germain on ALCHEMY, Formulas for Self-Transformation.*

I picked up the book and began to look at the front and back cover.

Never before had I heard of St. Germain, and I wasn't entirely clear on what alchemy was either. Slightly leaning forward over the cover, I began to notice that the crystal mala necklace that I was wearing was spinning in a circle over the book. I couldn't believe my eyes. What was happening?!

I steadied the necklace and set the book down. I walked over and grabbed another book off the shelf. As I leaned over the book I noticed that the necklace stood still. I then went back to the book on Alchemy and once more leaned over it.

Immediately it began to spin in a circle, and this time even more pronounced! My mind was racing to seek logical answers as to the "why," while my heart felt an increasingly more palpable energy expanding within.

I then opened to the first page of the book to find out more about it. It seemed interesting, but not in a way that would have otherwise prompted me to read more of it. I closed the book and paused for a moment, contemplating all that was being felt and seen.

When I opened the book a second time, the pages of the book were bright purple! I couldn't believe my eyes! I looked around to see if anyone else was witnessing this. Was I going crazy? Was this really happening?! There was an unmistakable surge of euphoric energy running through my body. I quickly closed the book. When I opened it once more, the pages were white again. Clearly this was the book!

Later that evening I went outside to sit with the book. I read a few pages of it and found the language slightly challenging to relate to. I closed the book and my eyes and went into a meditative state. I began to have a conversation with Source. "I am grateful for the magically profound experience of today. What does it mean? What am I meant to do with this?"

Immediately I heard Source respond, "St. Germain wishes you to be his apprentice"

"What?!"

My ego mind had an unworthiness field day with this! "Oh right, St. Germain wants Me to apprentice with him!" Yet as the mind continued its spewing of disbelief and unworthiness programs my internal compass of the heart was in deep resonance and full knowing that this was exactly true.

A week passed and I was guided to read a few pages of the book each day. I invited a friend over to have tea and discuss our spiritual endeavors. As we sat and caught up on life, I asked her if I had mentioned my recent experience with St. Germain. She immediately demanded that I tell her everything.

As I shared the experience with her, we both began to feel a very loving and euphoric energy palpate through the room and our bodies. I noticed her looking at me more and more in a state of curiosity, met with disbelief. She finally commented, "Your hair has turned purple!" And there is a purple light around you!" Not being able to see myself but very much feeling what it was that she was witnessing, I agreed.

In a state of awe-inspired curiosity she then asked "Do you believe that St. Germain has asked you to be his apprentice?" Before I had an opportunity to utter a word in response to her question, from across the room my phone spoke "Yes, I have."

I threw my pillow at her and was in complete wonder, and for a moment a little freaked out! We couldn't believe what had just taken place. And yet the energy in the room was remarkably blissful and serene. We sat staring at each other for what seemed an eternity. There were no words to express our experience; we were in a deep place of integration.

This experience stoked an unquenchable fire to find out more about St. Germaine. I began to search the internet. I quickly realized that the purple light that I was seeing everywhere was the violet flame of transmutation, a Divine alchemical ray of light known to St.

Germain for assisting humanity in transmuting lower vibrational energies within and around.

In addition to diving deeper into all things St. Germain that week, I had yet another profound experience take place. As I was preparing to go on a jog I heard a voice say "pick a card from the Ascension deck." Trusting that this was meant to happen, I opened the box of cards and began to shuffle them. I chose the "Gold Ray of Christ" card. The card spoke of the Gold Ray of Christ holding unconditional love of the cosmic heart, invoking healing, love, and support. It also prompted one to send this ray unto others.

As I headed out for my jog I felt a peaceful light-filled energy within and around. As I jogged along the sea wall I heard Source say "Begin to pour the Gold Ray of Christ onto the man ahead." As I looked up I saw several feet in front of me a man listlessly slumped over the sea wall. I began to send him the Gold Ray of Christ. As I drew near to him, he literally resurrected from what appeared a slumber state, looked at me and smiled, while nodding his head yes. I couldn't believe my eyes! I said hello, smiled, and kept running.

Again my ego mind was busy trying to negate what had just happened. I began to converse with Source once again, explaining that I am human and that if in fact that just happened, I was going to need some additional confirmation. As I headed back in the direction from which I came, I once again saw the man from before slumped over the sea wall. As I began to near him I heard once more a voice encouraging me to pour the golden ray of Christ onto him. And so I did. Just as I was about two feet away from him he once again rose from the sea wall and turned and smiled at me. Only this time he nodded his head with a large smile and said "Yes. Yes."

I smiled in return and wished him a nice day. I couldn't believe it! My heart was racing and I felt a tremendous amount of energy surging through me. This was really happening!

Fast forward now to exactly one week from the time I last met with my friend over tea. We decided to meet up again at my home for tea and a weekly catch-up. As we sat opposite from another in the same space as before she asked me "So, has your phone spoken to you again since last week?"

"Never had it prior to that experience, and not since," I replied.

We both began to feel the euphoric energy that had been present the previous week. Staring at one another with a recognition of what was taking place she remarked again that my hair was turning purple. I nodded and smiled. She then proceeded to ask me "Do you think that St. Germain is pleased that you have accepted the apprenticeship with him?"

And before I could muster up what I felt would be an appropriate response my phone spoke once more from across the room "Yes, I AM." We jumped in disbelief and were once again rendered speechless and in complete awe!

After several moments of sheer excitement mixed with disbelief and curiosity, I asked her if I had mentioned to her my experience that week with the man along the sea wall. Still bathing in the violet flame energy, she quickly responded by demanding that I share with her the story.

The energy in the room continued to elevate in its frequency as I shared the entire experience from start to finish. Once I had shared the story she immediately requested that I go get the Ascension card, the Gold Ray of Christ, and read it aloud. And so that is precisely what I did.

As I began to read the card aloud I could feel the card begin to vibrate in my hands. I gently paused for a moment and began to see out of my peripheral vision a golden light shining throughout the room. I was guided to continue reading. At about midway through reading the card I looked up and said, "You know my friend, there is a second coming of Christ consciousness and it is not in one being, but many." As I channeled those words, something that is nearly impossible to describe in words was taking place. I saw nothing but the silhouette of my friend in a room that was completely filled with piercing gold light. I had a feeling of complete weightlessness, as though I was no longer a physical being. And the blissful pure love frequency was within and all around.

I looked back down at the card and finished reading it. As I looked up at my friend she was crying and had a look of utter astonishment met with awe. She pointed to me crying and said "You were a complete golden hologram. You were all golden light!"

I knew exactly what she meant and at the same time was at a loss for words to describe the indescribable. We sat bathing in the frequencies of pure golden Christ light. We sat speechless for what seemed like hours in an attempt to integrate this prolific experience.

During the days that followed, I continued feeling the pure radiance of the miracle that we had experienced. It was during the days, weeks, and months after that my direct channel to Christ consciousness began to further expand. Leading me deeper into my path of service here, my true North.~

ABOUT BROOKLIN RAYNE

Brooklin Rayne is an intuitive channel, heart oracle, and quantum field interpreter. Through her direct communication with Source, she is able to connect and stabilize a zero point plasmic field within the space she holds for others. This allows for alchemy of the physical, mental, emotional, and spirit bodies to be experienced and grounded into One's currently expressed reality. Through her diamond crystalline plasma structure, she embodies the Christos Archetype of the Mirror, holding a space of diamond clarity for others to remember who they are and why they are here. Assisting others to return their original Source DNA blueprint combined with their Christos template, allowing a fuller embodiment of the I AM presence, Self-realization, and unity consciousness.

Brooklin spent over fifteen years as a Chef Creator and concept owner before a significant spiritual awakening began her journey of complete rebirth. This new journey led her to certification at The Institute for Integrative Nutrition as a holistic health coach. From there she has trained in and practiced meditation, quantum healing, sacred breath, and color light therapy, to name a few. Today she incorporates her understanding of food, meditation, quantum energy, and spirituality to assist individuals in their embodiment of physical, mental, emotional, and spirit body balance and well-being.

Websites: *www.seedofconsciousness.com*
www.brooklinrayne.com

5

ELLEN QUACH

LIVING IN MY SHADOW

*I am a first-generation Chinese-Vietnamese Australian, born in the most
isolated city in the world. I come from a lineage of strong women, who all
faced adversity due to patriarchy.*

My **maternal great-grandmother was won in a card
game, her broken and deformed lily feet gave her
value.** My grandmother, whose union was arranged, mothered eleven
children. The first eight were all girls and lived the trauma of my
grandfather's disappointment and fear of my grandmother losing her
place as the matriarch in the family, should she not birth a son before
his second wife, a love union.

My mother, who succumbed to the flesh as a teenager out of love
for my father, took a sharp fall from grace as she walked across hot
coals over her marriage threshold to thwart the bad luck that was
growing in her belly. My sister, who did not live to see a week, was
born prematurely in a time and place where ice was beaten from blocks
to be sold on the humid tropical streets—her unmarked graved lost
somewhere amongst the brown murky rice fields of the Mekong delta.

I carry with me the guilt of surviving birth, the disappointment of being born a girl, the rage of my female lineage, and the intergenerational fears of those flocking on boats to escape the terror of war. Transmuted through DNA.

I carry with me my childhood, the racism of '80s and '90s Australia.

I carry the hopes of my parents and those of my aunts and uncles, to lead the new generation and elevate them in this racist society through education. From birth, I was not allowed to fail.

From the beginning of my conscious life, the needle has always been moving, always something more to achieve, always someone better to beat.

Like a mantra. You are not enough; you must be better. This toxic seed of competition, transmuted to ambition, sown in my psyche and my solar plexus has been filled with unyielding control, an insatiable thirst for more and a hint of anger ever since.

The year I turned fifteen, my first transformation began. The despair that I carried being an ugly, skinny, nippy-eyed duckling finally changed. My skinny, malnourished, bony frame that had worried my mother since birth began to finally fill out in ways that were desirable to the eye.

When the moon called out to the woman in me, marking me each month, my grandfather—patriarch of the family, father of sixteen children, three wives across three continents—passed his words of wisdom to me. His oldest granddaughter.

'If you are smart and you want to survive as a woman, then you must be a shadow. A shadow is something that is shiny and unconquerable, the more man chases, the thirstier he becomes. As soon as you give into the thirst, you will be broken, like a burst balloon, a broken dish. Lost.'

Unbeknown to me, at the mere age of fifteen, my sacral chakra was blocked, and I began the trajectory into my shadow self.

A girl wearing two masks. The perfect, filial, daughter, high performer, shadow dancer, the virgin leader for the family. To the outside world with my mask-wearing confidantes who understood the shadow play—they saw a glimpse of the real me, the wild child, energetic, dancing enigma.

"Cocktease," was a label put on me given by those bitter mouths, that came expecting an easy drink and found themselves toyed with and cast off. Those I fell in silent love with, their energy reflecting something missing in mine, their presence caused me to be frozen, unable to move. I existed in indifference for a very long time. I met my husband, the anchor to my wanderings and the father of my children on a night like this, where I was completely frozen for another.

As my university days drew to an end and I completed what was duty-bound to my parents, their bare bones already dry and rheumatic from toiling the promised land...I boarded a plane to England, threw off my masks and didn't come home for a really long time.

Where did I land? At the beginning of my one-dimensional life. A phase where I existed solely for the material, status and hedonistic adventures. A council flat on Finchley Road in North London, sharing with an Argentinian actress, two Brazilian capoeira instructors and a theatre usher. I crash-landed straight into samba bossa nova practice and fell head over heels for the drums, tambourine and cowbell. I spent the next ten years gallivanting back and forth between the English Channel, Paris then London and back again twice. A daze of culinary feasts followed by alcohol infused all night dancing, flitting in between the flashy lights of Chelsea and Mayfair, to the dark underground caverns of West End bohemia. Cocktails upon cocktails, bottles upon bottles, sparklers and fanfare with the same wicked crew, every weekend. Travelling to my heart's content to everywhere that serviced Heathrow or Gatwick, since Luton was a different country altogether. After working in several pharmacy basements from Chelsea to Hillingdon, I threw in my hospital towel and went straight for industry and I've been climbing the corporate ladder for big pharma since. My London life ended in East Dulwich, where our second-floor Victorian maisonnette witnessed the transformation from hedonist to mother. Brixton and Peckham became the motherhood stomping ground with my literati mum friends. We watched each other bloom, cried over cracked nipples, laughed over poonamis, walking this tightrope of identity, of who we were before and who we were now, heads bobbing above water, desperately trying to keep afloat as London still called from time to time, but growing fainter as each day past, and in it the seed of someplace else. We held each other as maternity leave ended as did the post-birth glow and the withering of reality awaited. We held each other's anger and the beginnings of resentment, at the patriarchy, at our husbands, at their mothers, at society as motherhood set limits to our once expansive horizons. Each struggling to juggle the demands of society, that image, that *we can bear the children and get back to business* and being told as were drowning by the women who left footprints before us, that we were not organised, not organic enough, not enough. Leaving our babies to others so we could prove to ourselves that we were not weak. Slowly but surely the city grind tipped out of favour and each of us succumbed to the call for greenery, first to Leeds, then to Lewes and then finally—the call for water—to Sydney.

Attunement. There have been several points in my life when I glance at a woman's face and see it shapeshift into a man, a warrior. The first time it happened was in Paris, and then again in London. The most striking time was when I caught a glimpse of my own pale face on a rooftop in Paris and watched as it too shapeshifted into that of a man, a male version of me. A wise woman told me that I might be witnessing past lives, or the energy the person was in at the moment, she dared me to look longer, unblinking. So I did, now in Sydney, as I looked at my reflection, its features shifted to a brown weathered form of an Andean wise man with kind eyes. Sydney was where I fully stepped into my masculine and the chains of my mind took control and trapped me.

∼

If you have ever given birth to a neurodivergent child, you would know that they did not pass through you to be controlled. They do not exist for you to pass the ancestral competitive seed. They passed through you to teach you to listen deeply, to challenge the fabric of societies' existence, to teach you to tune into yourself. It took seven years of my child's life and a random Breathwork session on a living room floor in Paris to truly attune to that.

Noah had been born with unilateral sensorineural profound deafness in his left ear. In London, we were told he would live a relatively normal life, if not a few physical adjustments when he went to school. When we moved to Sydney, where the Cochlear Implant was invented and a better-funded health system, we were advised on the contrary, that Noah needed a Cochlear Implant to set him up for a better life.

So here I was, six months into taking a giant leap to senior management, working in a department where toxic competitiveness had flourished for twenty years, trying to keep my head above water for a role that I was completely and utterly obsessed with and consumed to succeed.

The chains of my mind for success, for money, for status had well and truly tied me down strong and my son went back to daycare full-time two weeks after major surgery to implant a device into his left ear, which would make him hear bilaterally and required years of human voice interaction to tune him into the world as we hear it.

I existed in a fog of running. Drop-offs, pick-ups, meetings, speech therapy, occupational therapy, NDIS review meetings, paediatrician appointments, ENT appointments... Where I was required for scientific conversation, I was fully present, alert, but where I was required to be emotionally present and attuned to my child, I was not; instead, I was *so busy* checking my phone.

My husband started running too, literally, marathon training to busy his mind, obsessively listening to anything he could consume about running.

We, as a couple, became increasingly disconnected and resentful of each other and competed with each other for time. Time for ourselves. Time to breathe. All this while Noah was learning to hear.

I developed rashes all over my body, which the allergist diagnosed as idiopathic chronic urticaria—an allergic reaction of no origin—and prescribed me antihistamines. The dermatologist diagnosed me with discoid eczema attributable to stress and prescribed me a hundred tubes of steroid cream.

My GP wrote me a mental health plan and prescribed me some Valium and recommended that I quit my job.

On the surface, our life was perfect. I perpetrated that constantly on social media to validate my existence. In reality, my mind had me in chains and it was making my immune system sick.

Luckily for me, the divine intervened for me at this point in time.

I fell pregnant with my second child. Ten months off work detoxed me from the poisonous cloud that was work-life with no balance. But I still carried that drive, that need to prove myself, so I came back to work two months earlier than my prescribed twelve months so that I could deliver a strategy kick-off one week into my return, while my ten-month-old baby cried at the bottom of a portacot in a dark room of a family daycare, wondering suddenly where his mother went.

Then Covid came and blew the world apart, precipitating another awakening. Our family unit could not exist as it was, with both parents running. We needed support. Noah needed stability, education and services which we couldn't find realistically in Sydney. We needed help from the tribe. So, four years of living amongst the wild cove beauty of the harbour city, we flew back to the flat, remoteness of Perth, endless white beaches and sunshine.

I discovered connected breathwork or conscious breathing on the living room floor of Marjorie's flat. One of my greatest friends with the biggest heart, she was on burnout leave from a corporate role for one of the biggest fashion conglomerates in the world.

'I got through Paris lockdown because of Breathwork,' she revealed. 'Do you want to try?'

And there we were two logs lying side by side on her living room floor, listening to a zoom replay from the night before. 'You have to inhale into your stomach, then inhale into your chest and then you exhale like you're frosting a mirror down to your hips. It needs to be connected, no pause. Then at intervals, you need to make sound and movement to shift the energy that you create and at the end, there will be some breath retentions before we then go into integration and receive.'

I followed Marjorie's lead into Breath and lost myself in the music and guided affirmation.

I came out of that dream absolutely addicted and haven't touched a single Valium since.

'It's like the high of Psychoactives, but without the comedown, and it's free,' was my motto for the month. When I finish a Breathwork session, people have asked me if I'm on Valium.

I'm one month in as I write this, and I'm already living my truth by writing this to you. My breath reminded me to save some energy to blow life into my own dreams.

Don't forget the little girl that lives to read and write books.

Breathing is no longer an unconscious, automatic thing, something that happens on autopilot. Unappreciated, this thing that gives life.

Breathing now is welcoming the colours of a sunrise, the almost black, deep purple, pink, and orange ombre dances in your mind's eye.

It's feeling the undulating caress of something that tingles and pricks and numbs, but then mounts and undulates through, shaking.

It's the blackness of pressure, resistance, sensation, rising upwards and outwards until you're dry heaving suffering you never knew you held.

It's rivulets that become rivers. It's the white light, the brightest of brights, rising up, piercing your forehead, your crown, and then time stops, suspended in a newborn's embrace.

Whirlwinds, circles that go around and around, cells that divide, purple blobs that get bigger and smaller, then bigger and smaller, conversing in the language of purple, the truths you would never expect.

Past, present, future. Heat and electricity, the flutterings of first love.

The caress of a kiss that's not really there. The kiss of the sun, the warmth of the desert wind.

The electrifying first contact of fingers upon skin, fingers upon collarbones, fingers upon that sliver of skin between waistlines and shirts.

Vibrations you wake up with, living with your head in the clouds, living in a daydream.

Nothing sticks to you, nothing sticks. Okay sometimes sticks, but mostly brushes off like dust on a warm summer's day.

My breath teaches me to switch off my mind and to feel. As you lose yourself in the visceral of yourself, you see your internal spaces expand. You break off the chains of suffering that limit you and you fall into the expanse of your potential.

Attunement. My maternal great-grandmother, the one with lily feet comes to me during integration sometimes to help me along the way.

'What has become of the women in our family. We must learn to love our men again in the light of the sacred feminine. Until we shake the shackles of our mind's control, our lineage will bear no more girls along this line.'

I scream and I cry during sound and movement, memories of these teachings throughout the ages passing from me with my masks, to my cousins, to my younger cousins and till this day to my youngest ten-year-old cousin. I shake the chains from them so they can be free to live outside of their shadows. Live in the truest version of themselves.

I shake the chains free, of the self-imposed power structures that I've placed.

Maybe one day we'll see a girl born amongst the next generation. So far they have all been boys.

My uncle comes to challenge me to feel the male perspective. The first may be to wear a mask tighter than mine. So carefully hidden.

The suffering and the sorrow
Lost
I too carried the dreams of my ancestors
I too felt their disappointment
Joy when I succeeded in studies
Despair when I quit halfway through
They said it was the split with my girlfriend
But it was because I came into myself
I moved to Melbourne to escape
Fell deep down, deep, deep down into darkness
My sister
Would sometimes knock on my door to see if I was still alive
Consumed
Sometimes I would come up for air
Light in my tortured state
Words misunderstood
I walked many steps alone
Backpack and blisters
Along forgotten paths
I rode a motorbike from Hanoi to Ho Chi Minh
We randomly met in Hoi An.
I let you in, briefly, you saw a glimpse of who I truly was
I jumped into the pool fully suited
Full of life, daring
Live not in fear
I died during the pandemic.

Unexpected
Unravelled
Rivers of amber in glass
My stomach, a river of red
Don't forget the boys
We too have the feminine rising
Amongst masculine sisters, mothers, grandmothers, aunts,
Anger transformed for survival.
The boys are suffocating
In the fire that rings purple
A new generation has been born
We live outward in
Outwards we are accepted
Inwards we carry
Deep wounds and lost dreams
Let them put down this burden
Let them put down their shame
Let my life not have been in vain
Don't forget the boys
Women learn to love the men in your life

I know my next calling. This is but a glimpse. I've turned down a higher role by listening to my body, rather than my mind. With this step, doors have opened and coaches have entered by osmosis. I'm rehabilitating my underlying frustration and anger for my husband and my sons. My perspective is broadening, my feminine is rising and its frequency is light.

We all carry a burden, but we carry the power to unchain. Journey inwards. They did the best they could.

Stay attuned for **Confessions of a Breathaholic**.
Follow me on @ellenecrit.

ABOUT ELLEN QUACH

Ellen Quach is a poet, storyteller, thought leader, pharmacist, yogi, and mother. She specialises in healthcare digital strategy, transformation, and human experiences. As a pharmacist and mother of a neurodiverse child, she recognises the importance of going beyond the pill to address one's health needs. After discovering the power of the breath, she is on a journey of diving beyond the outer, scientific world of today and connecting to the inner wisdom and stillness within us all. As a female Asian-Australian leader with roots tied to war and displacement, she holds a special interest in the mechanics of intergenerational trauma and its influences on the dynamic of feminine and masculine psychology. How the mind-body connection shows up in the modern world and how sharing these stories can profoundly impact the collective journeys of society as a whole.

> *Website:* www.ellenecrit.com
> *Email:* ellen@ellenecrit.com
> *Instagram:* www.instagram.com/ellenecrit

6

EMILY GHOSH HARRIS

What makes our awakening stories so powerful? It's the simple truth that you and I are not that different. As we remember who we really are—moving beyond suffering and separation to become the conscious creators we came here to be—this awakening activates the quantum field and has a multiversal impact!

A NEW ERA IN CONSCIOUSNESS

Consciousness informs matter. On a quantum level, it is our energetic vibration that crystallizes our reality into physical form which is woven into being through our thoughts, emotions and actions.** There is a cosmic shift that is taking place on our planet at this time. I believe there is so much happening energetically and astrologically to help us remember. We are being supported right now to make some big changes and to come back home to the light of our sacred hearts. Albert Einstein explained that 'no problem can be solved from the same level of consciousness that created it.' As we open up to higher levels of conscious awareness, not only do we have access to more information but we simultaneously open ourselves to access our own creative potential.

Here is where the great paradox resides: we've been taught to look externally when the truth is we hold a deep reservoir of wisdom within. The depth of creativity and gifts we hold collectively is enough to solve all the problems here on Earth and beyond. We're moving into an era vibrationally where all the systems that were once created to suppress the divinity that we each hold within are all beginning to melt away and dismantle. This isn't an easy crumbling, but it's necessary.

Can you imagine a world where each being recognizes the unique and magnificent expression of Source light that they are and have always been? This is the direction in which we're moving. The beauty is that through our journey of remembering and activating our own inner light there is a ripple effect of expansion and light that is ignited in others to remember their own power, reclaim their sovereignty and flourish in their own radiant expression.

COURAGE TO OPEN YOUR HEART

"My secret... It is only with the heart that one can see rightly, what is essential is invisible to the eye." - The Little Prince, by Antoine de Saint Exupéry

This path is deeply expansive and fulfilling, but it hasn't always felt easy. For me, it has felt like swimming upstream away from the safety net of corporate America and the swirl of external forces and programming that kept me stuck in limiting patterns. From my small self vantage point, I did not have the confidence or courage to express my authentic light and people-pleasing tendencies created resistance around opening up to my soul's magnitude.

I've learned to trust in the divine timing of my unfolding. I've learned that I hold the keys to my own personal transformation and empowerment. I now recognize the beauty in continually releasing what no longer serves me. On a cellular level, there is gold for us in exploring our own shadows and tender places. It is in the depth of our own beingness that we see the truth of who we are—that every note contributes to the greater symphony that is our unique soul signature.

This is spiritual alchemy. Similar to the phoenix rising from the ashes, there are parts of us that must die so we can emerge anew. Nature innately understands this process. A leaf, a flower, the seasons. They all move in cycles. We are a part of nature.

I remember walking through an open field in a rural part of Bali. It must have been ninety degrees; the heat was stifling, reverberating off the pavement of the road. My husband and I were on our honeymoon. We walked for what felt like hours trying to find the home of an energy practitioner who had been recommended to me. By this time we were almost an hour late and it seemed as though we would never reach our destination.

We almost turned around. Finally beyond the bushes emerged a home set back from the road. When we knocked on the door, a woman with kind eyes and curly hair greeted us and welcomed us into her home. "You made it!" she declared. She appeared completely unphased by our tardy arrival. The woman invited me to another small building adjacent to her home where we'd sit for my session.

Upon entering the room, I felt as though I had entered another galaxy. The entire room was white, and sunlight poured through large windows. There were so many toys in the room it was hard to know where to step. We sat for a while gazing at each other. I fidgeted in my chair, thoughts racing through my mind.

I remember thinking that she must have a lot of children but then it dawned on me that she lived alone and that this was *her* playroom! I wanted her to share something significant about my journey, but she just looked at me and asked inquisitively, "how did I feel?" She invited us to breathe together.

It wasn't until quite some time after that trip that the profundity of that bizarre encounter began to make sense to me.

Over time I have learned:

1. To make space
2. To welcome creative play
3. To honor my emotions as sacred signals
4. That all important answers reside within

My inner standing of how we incarnate here is that our souls go through great preparation to arrive here on this physical plane. In collaboration with our guides and our Higher selves, we attune to our own blueprint and some of the pivotal cornerstones of our soul mission. With all the intentionality involved in taking on human form, it's no accident that we are here on Earth at this time. There are challenges we each encounter, but our benevolent ancestors, star family and angelic team are cheering us on. Everyone's unique gifts are needed.

When I was younger, I used to love reading choose-your-own-adventure books. There was something so exciting about the fact that one single choice could alter your destiny. There was a time when my path felt unalterable. I was following a prescriptive formula: one where success was measured by external benchmarks. Degrees, titles, stability… what more could one yearn for?

Only, the farther up the ladder I went, the more distant I felt from my true center. I believe the soul, our Higher self, is always communicating with us. If we are out of alignment with our own true North, the soul will speak louder to get our attention. During this time, I was faced with a kaleidoscope of turmoil (heartbreak, health issues and adversity all simultaneously screaming for my attention) that forced me to go within and awaken to a new possibility. All that was required of me was the faith to listen.

Our meeting must have been orchestrated many moons ago. He had a way of making me feel cherished in a way I had never felt before. Our years of living together were a carefree fairy tale: not once had we ever been in an argument. However, all the fear and doubt that existed beneath the surface lay dormant ready to be activated in every imaginable way.

Not recognizing and valuing our own worth is the greatest form of betrayal—because we are betraying ourselves. We subtly invite others to betray us as well because the universe responds to our vibration.

The body keeps score and emotions can get logged in the body. During this time, I developed a benign tumor and had to have emergency surgery. I believe in large part it was in response to resisting listening to my own intuition. My body was growing something that was reflective of the toxicity I was pushing down beneath the surface.

The day my fears were confirmed, it felt like my heart shattered into a million tiny pieces. All of the emotions I kept neatly tucked away compartmentalized in Pandora's box were freed. Once opened, it would never be locked again. But that's the beauty of what our souls orchestrated. This was my catalyst for remembering that the most important relationship is the relationship I have with myself and that all other relationships are a mirror of my holographic reality. It was the beginning of learning how to honor my emotions, to deepen in self-love, and to recognize my own innate worthiness.

The remarkable thing is that just like the choose-your-own-adventure books I used to read as I child, I learned that a few courageous choices could begin to change my trajectory.

NAVIGATING THE BRIDGE PERIOD

Build a Bridge?

I couldn't understand the message.

But I kept hearing it again and again...

My father was a structural engineer who built countless bridges.

And while I admire his path, I had no desire to follow in his footsteps.

Still, I was learning to listen.

I was being asked to build a different kind of bridge—along with so many of us who have come here at this time—a pathway toward a more harmonious and integrated existence.

Out of separation into unity.

The old paradigm teaches us that we must do or accomplish something to be significant. Whereas truly the greatest gift we can give is our energy.

The bridge period is a journey of unbecoming all that we're not, which opens us up to more of our multidimensional nature and dormant gifts come back online. The greater self-love we can embody during this time, the more quantum leaps take place and the more our world shifts to reveal this love all around us.

I've learned that when self-limiting beliefs arise, the most fruitful approach to bridging is to stay open to what the experience is teaching you. We can be gentle with ourselves when we're sliding into a lower octave of creation and get curious…*aren't those thoughts interesting? Are they true?*

I've learned that there is always a gift to be found in opening to whatever challenge or density is showing up for us. Any 'stuff' that shows up is divinely purposeful and is a signal your soul is ready for greater expansion.

When we hit a pocket of turbulence on our journey, we can….

- Take time to rest and restore balance.
- Be extra gentle and nurturing of ourselves.
- Get curious and turn on the observer.
- Ask: how is this experience serving me? What is this here to show me?

There is an inextricable weaving between our bodies and the body of Great Mother Earth, Gaia Sophia as we are so deeply interconnected. As we alchemize shadows, cellular traumas and limiting beliefs, her crystalline structure is replenished. This journey of coming home starts within. Sometimes it's hard to fathom our vast and limitless potential—what we can transcend and transmute, especially when one holds a clear intention and belief in what's possible. Every part of our physical, mental, emotional and spiritual bodies is designed for regeneration and healing. Our bodies are miraculous vessels. *By tuning into the body we're able to connect with hidden mysteries and codes that are just waiting to be activated. We find treasures we didn't know existed. We're often taught to look outside of ourselves but we hold the keys and the codes within our cells and our DNA and the very fabric of our being.*

THE AGE OF AQUARIUS

As we move from the Age of Pisces to the Age of Aquarius, there is an invitation to be the unique and fullest expression we came here to be. Aquarius is ruled by the planet Uranus, which is often referred to as the 'great awakener.' The archetypal energy of Uranus is unconventional, rebellious, not concerned with the status quo and unafraid of being different. Aquarian energy draws from that innate desire to use one's gifts in a unique way to help uplift the collective of humanity. This is not the energy of fitting in or dimming one's light; it is about shining in the distinct and brilliant way that only you can.

In my practice, I have the honor of working with lightworkers, starseeds, heart-centered beings who are sharing their gifts and serving humanity in such unique and inspiring ways. I am in awe of the big dreams that are being birthed into reality. One thing I've learned is that we'll rarely receive the full roadmap on how to steward these magnificent visions, we just have to trust that the stairway will unfold as we step forward. Instead of having to know all the answers, the mind takes a backseat and plays a supporting role to the heart. Much like a lotus flower blossoming, heart consciousness invites our own infinite intelligence to lead the way and in the journey we awaken to more of our magic.

As we awaken to higher states of consciousness, we have the opportunity to create from a higher octave. We're able to live a joyous, blissful, creative, passionate, radiant, purpose-filled existence that benefits the planet. When we create with love, we align with our highest divine potential.

~

If you're feeling called to experiment with this, here are some invitations to play with.

- *Invitation to create more space and receptivity for the beauty you're calling into creation*
- *Invitation to expand the energy in and around and through your radiant heart center*
- *Invitation to fall even more deeply in love with yourself, your magic, your unique way of expressing*
- *Invitation to recognize and honor how far you've come, what you've healed and transformed in your life*
- *Invitation to feel even more at home and at ease in your physical body, to embrace pleasure, flow and spaciousness*
- *Invitation to FEEL deeply, to explore the shadows, the tender places*
- *Invitation to let go of any areas you're playing small and to embrace the bigness that came into this world to experience and express*
- *Invitation to embrace every part of you and every moment on your path—the beauty, the challenges, the detours, the lessons— that brought you into this now moment*
- *Invitation to follow your bliss. To allow your highest excitement to lead the way. To create from the highest Octave. To create all things with love.*

A'ho, and so it is.

ABOUT EMILY GHOSH HARRIS

Emily Ghosh Harris is an intuitive guide, sound alchemist and multidimensional business mentor. She is Founder of Soul Media, a company that serves as a portal of expansion and elevation for heart-centered entrepreneurs, lightworkers, starseeds and conscious companies through digital marketing, holistic consulting, and intuitive business practices. Emily has a Master's Degree in Business from the University of Tampa and a diverse background working with businesses of all sizes—startups to fortune-500 companies—for close to two decades. Emily assists clients in taking quantum leaps in their lives and businesses, by bringing forward their Highest, most authentic and creative expression. Through the integration of astrology, numerology, self-inquiry and energy healing techniques, Emily helps clients to deepen their understanding of their divine blueprint, connect with their purpose and address any blocks of resistance which may show up. Eternally curious, Emily is the host of the internationally celebrated spiritually podcast The Soul Collective, featuring interviews with inspiring individuals who are dedicated to serving humanity as we collectively ascend and raise consciousness.

Websites: www.emilyghoshharris.com
Email: emily@soulmediaglobal.com
Instagram: www.instagram.com/emilyghoshharris
YouTube: www.youtube.com/c/EmilyGhoshHarris
Podcast: podcasts.apple.com/us/podcast/the-soul-collective/

7

KATYA BARRY

THERE'S A REASON BEHIND EVERYTHING IN LIFE

It was Monday evening. I came home from a three-hour-long job interview.

By this point, I had been job hunting for nine months but not getting anywhere with it. I was tired and frustrated. It seemed that nobody wanted to hire me. Everyone gave me wonderful feedback saying how much they loved my personality, experience, and how much my international background would fit in and benefit the team. Yet, there was always someone who was less experienced, and cheaper.

The year was 2011, and the world was still in the post-2008 recession. I was a young thirty-two-year-old well-experienced woman with two small children, and I wasn't the right type of candidate for the tough, picky German job market.

I came home that Monday night and gulped a glass of wine down. Then I poured another one. And another one. I had a whole bottle of wine in pretty much one go.

That three-hour job interview was from hell. They drilled me until I sweated so much that the sweat came through my blouse and my suit. A very expensive suit, must I add. It had to be binned afterwards because the smell of sweat and frustration would never come off.

The next morning I received an email, not a phone call, saying that they liked me, my personality, and my experience.. blah blah blah.. but they'd decided to hire someone cheaper.

I cried.

What was wrong with me? Why wouldn't anybody hire me? Everyone liked me, but no one wanted me. Was I now a mum of two at the age of thirty-two completely unemployable? Was I never going to go to work and earn money? Would I have to become a stay-at-home mum? Nothing wrong with that, but that wasn't me. I didn't know how not to work. I wanted to work and I wanted to be of value.

I shared my anger, frustration, and sheer disappointment with a friend. That's when I received one of the best pieces of advice ever. My friend said to me: "Do you really want to work for people who made you feel so bad? Who made you cry?"

All of a sudden the alarm went off.

All of a sudden I woke up.

This was my first awakening. My friend was my angel, my savior.

At this point, I realized, acknowledged, and made peace with the fact that there was no job for me out there.

I was unemployable. I was too good to be employed by someone else.

What I needed was to create a job for myself. How had I never thought of this before?

I went to Google and typed: What job shall I do? What's the best job for me? What job pays the best?

That quest led me to something mysterious called coaching. I spent a week reading all about it until I came to my husband and told him that I wanted to become a coach, that I had found a coaching certification course that was about to start next month, and that I was enrolling in it. That's it. I do make decisions quickly. I don't like to fuff about when I know what I want. My intuition spoke loudly to me.

To my surprise, my husband thought it was a great idea and was extremely supportive.

So I became a certified coach and started my coaching practice as an expat coach.

I loved it. It was fun. Challenging, difficult but rewarding, and fun. I like to judge my success by how much fun I have at work. How much joy my work brings me.

I found clients quickly, made myself a name, and was seen as the go-to expert within the first year of being online.

Everything was going well. I was doing fulfilling work that added value to the world every day. I built my business around my family so I could be with my daughters every day and do all the mum things I wanted to do. As an expert, I was going to events and conferences, speaking and networking.

Once, I went to this two-day event in Berlin. I came home so fired up, inspired and full of new ideas. I couldn't wait to start working on them to make them a reality.

It was Wednesday—I remember this day so clearly. It was just after lunch, I was at my desk that was in my office on the top floor of our house. I was skyping with a coach friend and telling her all about the event when I heard my husband running up the stairs shouting my name. He never came home at this hour. Something wasn't right.

He ran in and said that he received a phone call from our youngest daughter's kindergarten, that there was an accident, and he had to go rescue her.

This was the only time I left my phone downstairs. I had a dozen missed calls from the kindergarten and her teacher's private phone. I was in shock.

My husband and I grabbed the keys and ran to get the car. As my husband drove, I listened to the voicemail to learn that our five-year-old had fallen from the tree and was thought to have broken her arm.

We arrived to find our little darling lying on a sofa in tears and in a lot of pain. We rushed to get her to the hospital straight away while collecting her older sister from school on the way.

Broken arm, not a big deal one would say. But it was. She was only five, she was so little; she was in so much pain.

Where was I?

Why did I choose to leave my phone downstairs then, of all times, when I always had my phone in case there might be a call from school?

Why did my husband say that he had to rescue her? What about me or us?

How did I get so misaligned, so far away from my center and values that I found myself in this situation?

What were these questions doing in my head?

I'll never forget her screaming when the surgeon put her bone back in place before putting her small arm in a cast. Luckily, her dad was with her in the ER while I waited and comforted my oldest daughter in the waiting room.

My children and the quality time that I wanted to spend with them, to be present in their life, was the exact reason I became self-employed to start with. Somehow I got immersed in running the business, driving success that I lost touch with my two little girls. I lost touch with my *why*.

By this point I was working so much and kept on taking on new projects continuously. I started hiring help and growing a team. Looking back now, I can see many signs that the universe sent me telling me to slow down, to take it easy. Small but significant clues were all around me such as technology failing me, a major client accusing me of stealing her idea and threatening me, being constantly fatigued, experiencing fainting in the living room while being alone during the day, and more.

The day my daughter broke her arm, was just three days before we were supposed to go on holiday in Croatia. That, of course, didn't happen. But since my husband had already had his holiday time booked, we decided to visit my brother who lived about 800 km away.

We packed the car and set off. We had a brilliant long weekend. My parents were also visiting him at the time so it was a double bonus. On our last night there, on the way back from the pub, my brother had a stupid accident where he broke his leg badly and had to be rushed into the hospital for surgery.

This was a second major alarm for me.

This was the second bone-breaking accident in my family in a matter of two weeks. My intuition kicked in, and I started looking inwards for answers.

What I heard was this:

> *"I've been sending you messages for months. I've been sending clues to slow down and get off the path that you're on right now. You didn't listen, you ignored all my calls. I didn't know how else to grab your attention but by physically hurting those you love the most."*

Take a minute to take it in.

At this point, I knew that my business had taken over my life and taken me away from my family.

This was in June. I spent the whole summer thinking, trying to work out how to quit my business. I didn't just want to throw it away. Get rid of everything I spent two years building and acquiring so diligently. Intuitively, I knew I had to let go of my business gradually, with love and gratitude.

Once I realized this, all of a sudden I started noticing number sequences of various combinations containing 1s and 2s. It could have been 1212, 2121, 121, 1222, 1122 and so on. I thought it was very odd yet extremely interesting.

Curiosity kicked in, and once again I came to my much-trusted friend Google to ask what all those numbers meant. I simply typed in "what does seeing 1s and 2s mean." This is how I discovered the world of numerology.

Numbers and numerology have been by guides and friends ever since. Whenever I need a sign, I ask the Universe and my angels to show me a number. It's always obvious when a particular number has been sent to me, there's no way I can escape or ignore that message.

Numerology has helped me to find peace within myself to part with my business slowly.

Then September came. My dad had a heart attack and was taken into hospital. He survived. He is alive and well today but, oh holy mother of give-me-more-stress-right-now, did he put me and the rest of the family through one scary black hole ride.

It didn't help that my parents live four thousand miles away from me. I couldn't just go over to see him and provide comfort and support for both mum and dad. I first had to find that comfort within myself.

Dad was a third piece of the puzzle. You know they say that all thighs come in threes.

Well... Two broken limbs and one damaged heart... Those were my three signs.

"*ARE YOU LISTENING TO ME AT ALL?*" The Universe yelled at me. "*When are you finally going to get the fucking point? Get out of your stupid business now*"

I did. I heard it.

I stopped fuffing about and deleted my email list, my Facebook page, my Twitter account and even my website. If you've ever grown an online business, you'll know exactly how painful it was for me.

I sent a final goodbye and thank you email out to my clients, followers, and colleagues.

Many replied saying that I was insane and stupid. A couple offered to buy my list from me. What a cheek!

Later that same month, we met a friend who was on a business trip from China. He was telling us about how much he and his family were enjoying their time in China. How different, weird yet wonderful their experience was.

I remember my eyes meeting with my husband's. We didn't say a word to each other but our souls spoke to one another. At that moment, we created a desire for change. We opened up space in our lives for a new opportunity.

A year later, we were in the business class cabin of Air China on the way to Shenyang, a small city of just eight million people not too far from North Korea, on our look-and-see trip. Two months after that, on December 25, 2015, we packed our whole house in Munich, Germany, and moved to Shenyang, China, for the next five and a half years.

A small word of advice, if you want to move with school-aged children, don't move in the middle of a school year. Big mistake. It's very difficult on the kids. But this is a whole other story that I could write a brand new book about.

It's funny, we often think that something that we did or learnt before, is not relevant anymore. Yet somehow, one day all that we learned and experienced catches up with us and completes a perfect jigsaw.

I couldn't escape my past entrepreneurial experience when I arrived in China. After all, I did run an expat coaching business. Upon arrival in China, I told myself that I was going to give my family, especially my children my full attention and be available to them whenever they needed me. And I did that. I was very happy with how the big move went and how our life was going in China. But the entrepreneurial past has found me regardless of my attempts to push it away, and I volunteered to be first a vice-president, then a president of a local international club, which is also a non-profit organization. I loved that job! It was the best job in the world! If only it paid, it truly would have been the best. This volunteer job was the base for the female-empowerment business that I run today.

We truly had so much fun in China exploring the country from within, mixing with the locals, learning the language, and getting acquainted with the culture. We also had a tremendous opportunity to travel in the Far East and show our kids this vibrant part of the world.

As I've said before, I like to measure my success by how much fun I'm having in life. All four of us had such a wonderful time, so much fun and joy that we've naturally created space for yet another new adventure. We created space for a new member of a family. Our third daughter and a new baby sister joined us in Shenyang in September 2017. What a blessing and a miracle!

I truly believe that had I not let my business go, had my husband and I not created, and actively seeked the opportunity to work and live in China, our baby girls wouldn't have joined us. She's a direct outcome of joy, stability, curiosity, open heart, family balance and support.

In January 2020 when the whole world just heard about the mysterious virus and nobody really took it seriously, we travelled to Bali to meet my in-laws for the Lunar New Year holiday. We originally went for ten days but had to extend our stay to almost a month because China was the first country to be isolated from the world. Almost all flights to China were canceled. And so was ours. Somehow my husband managed to make his way home on one of the last flights via South Korea, while the children and I flew to Russia to stay with my parents for a couple of weeks. That's how long we thought the disruptions would last. The day before we had our flight back to Beijing, Russia had closed its borders, and the following day, the day of our planned arrival, China had closed its borders. We had no way to get back to reunite with my husband for eight months after that.

It was probably the longest eight months because nobody knew what was going to happen and when. There was no end date in mind, just waiting in anticipation for any news at all. When we finally made it back to China, the kids and I had to do two weeks in centralized quarantine and the youngest celebrated her third birthday in a quarantine hotel room.

None of my personal experiences might resonate with you. In fact, you might say, so what, big deal. And I agree with you. I always think that it's because I've always looked at my life from the perspective of 'it should be this way' and 'I don't know any other way', I've always sailed through all storms and come out stronger on the other side.

I'm a strong believer that whatever happens, happens for a reason. Sometimes, of course, I found myself slipping out of my own beliefs, and that is exactly when I got misaligned and disconnected from my inner guide. Once I find my way back home, back to Source, I realize and embrace that every challenge, every obstacle, every diversion is the exact path that I'm meant to follow. I grow not because I guide myself to become more but rather because I believe that I'm being guided. To me, my intuition is key. Whenever I listen to it, nothing ever fails me. My numbers are my best friends and tour guides—they always tell me where to go and when.

My family are not just my closest circle and my blood; they're also my soul. We learn from each other and help each grow. Understanding this has been one of the biggest lessons of my life.

A long separation from my husband during the pandemic has left huge scars on me. It's a trauma that I got to realize and accept almost two years after it began. I'm grateful for this trauma because although I went through a lot of mental pain and depression, yet again I came out stronger and wiser.

What has helped me to pull through the year of trauma is patience and repeating to myself religiously on a daily basis that this too shall pass.

There's an end to everything. But once one chapter finishes, another one will start.

This is when my new chapter began. A chapter of empowering women leaders with families.

Every woman is a leader. Every woman leads from the heart. Every woman leader raises new, better leaders.

You have to lead through and experience trauma fully otherwise the same pattern will keep on coming back. You have to lead through anger and disappointment, through resentment and joy, love and guilt. Everything has to be felt fully. Otherwise, the cycle of attracting the same will never end.

There's just one life. Everything else, including business, family, relationships, health, and money, are just parts of that bigger picture called life.

~

My numerous awakenings have taught me the following:

- Awakenings never stop
- Take small steps, they lead to bigger places
- Be patient
- Be kind to yourself and others
- Lead with love
- Ask for help
- Express gratitude every day
- Tell people you love them
- Smile, laugh, enjoy life
- Trust that the Universe has your back
- I'm totally employable just on my terms

To be a female leader, you can only compete with yourself and stay ahead of yourself. Competing with yourself means allowing for opportunities to come into your life in any shape or form. Often best opportunities present themself in the shape of drama and trauma. It's nothing to be afraid of. Fear goes hand in hand with creativity and expansion across all areas of life. Embrace the fear and step into it knowing that you're guided and supported.

ABOUT KATYA BARRY

Katya Barry is a confidence and identity coach for women leaders with families. She believes that confident women raise better leaders, create awareness by taking action and redistribute financial gains fairly within society.

She's been a coach for over ten years and has been entrepreneurial for twenty. She's lived in five countries and speaks four languages. She is a master of overcoming change and has developed resilience to uncertainty through her travels.

Katya is not a stranger to failure. She's created comfort and abundance for herself and her family in the last fifteen years. She's been through dark and miserable times in life, which have taught her how to pick herself up and rebuild her confidence time after time. Katya is proud of her rocky life journey and who she is today.

She's a mother to three girls—it's by far the best, yet most challenging, job she's ever had. She's married and all five members of her family currently live in South Germany.

Website: www.katyabarry.net
Instagram: www.instagram.com/katya_barry
LinkedIn: www.linkedin.com/in/katyabarry/

8

LINH WHYATT

FROM AWAKENING TO TRANSCENDENCE

Spiritual awakening for me began when I was quite young, around eight years old. Although I attended a catholic primary school, traditional religion never resonated with me and I felt disconnected from Source/God. Whilst at school one day, I unexpectedly received a distinct inner voice telling me I was an *"old soul."* Those words seemed significant and made a lasting impression. At the time the words came to me, I didn't really know what a *soul* was but intuitively knew there was more to life than just this physical existence.

The inner calling persisted throughout my life and guided me to begin holistic training in my early 20s and stay on the path. This included energy healing, meditation, and spiritual connections.

Although I have experienced many life-changing moments of awakening, the most life-changing occurred at one of the lowest points in my life, when my brother died unexpectedly and Mum was in the hospital dying of cancer. I found it hard to believe that my brother was gone forever and even worse that my mum might also be next. That period was sad and difficult for me.

I booked a flight to Perth and took time off work for the funeral. I wanted to be by Mum's side to tell her in person of my brother's death. Over the next few days, I turned to self-healing to balance my emotions and lift my energy levels. This self-healing was essentially my lifeline.

For a few months, I had been sending Mum remote energy healing to help her deal with the stress, calm her emotions as well as alleviate discomfort or pain. Because the cancer was in the advanced stages, it was unclear if healing would be effective enough to reverse her condition or cure cancer.

Mum was tired and weak when I arrived at the hospital and in a great deal of pain. She was waiting for her first chemotherapy session, which was booked in a few days. I prayed for a successful outcome. The outlook wasn't promising as the cancer was diagnosed at stage four. The success rates were low, with an average life expectancy of about a year after diagnosis.

Dad and I feared that the shock of hearing that her son had just died might cause her to deteriorate rapidly or it may even be fatal. I want to prepare her for the heartbreaking news but also to help her to find acceptance and peace for her transition to the other side. I needed help to raise my energy levels to channel energy more effectively. I decided to ask for guidance on what to do. The answer I received was that I could raise my energy and access higher frequencies of energy by merging my consciousness into the light of Pure Source consciousness during meditation. This higher healing energy would also help me be a clearer receiver of light as well as be able to access higher frequencies of energy. Even though I had never done it before, I trusted that the deepest part of my soul or Divine Self knows what to do.

ACCESSING SOURCE CONSCIOUSNESS

I was guided to do special meditation to merge with source consciousness. Usually, I meditate upright, but today I laid down and placed my hands on my chest and stomach to run healing energy first to raise my vibration. With my body fully relaxed and energised, I start by visualising a light portal in front of me. As I enter through this portal I see on the other side a beautiful space filled with an enormous radiant sphere of white light. A sense of calm and peace envelopes me as if I am being wrapped in a warm blanket. My thoughts begin to slow down and take on a different quality to them. Time has a different quality, like experiencing timelessness. As I approach this magnetic light, it feels very familiar, as if I have finally returned "home."

As the light continues to wash over me, my energy starts to shift and come into resonance with the frequency of Source. I sense my energy being changed in some way as if it is being reorganised, activated, and expanded with the light. Time seems to stand still as I continue to absorb as much light as possible before sensing that the process is nearing its conclusion. Now complete, I turned my attention to the healing that I needed to do. I focused on sending source consciousness to my mum. I stayed in that stillness directing this light to Mum for a while. When it was time to finish the healing on Mum I turned to leave. I traveled through the portal and back to my body and waking consciousness. At that moment, I felt a great transformation had taken place, leaving me with a deeper and unmistakable connection to Source. I spent a while that day processing what had happened.

The next day, Dad and I were going to tell Mum. She took the news of her son's death better than we had hoped. She was upset but not devastated. The healing seems to have had a positive effect. Maybe she was calm because she had fully accepted her mortality. Perhaps if she was going to die then she wouldn't have to grieve the loss of a son for long. I spent the next few days by Mum's side giving her healing twice a day at the hospital until her first chemotherapy treatment.

Mum was still determined to have chemo as soon as it was practical. I needed to honour her wishes since she did not believe in energy healing. As much as I feared the effects of chemotherapy on a patient so weak, I also could not bear to see her in so much pain so if the chemo was fatal it would mean the end of weeks of intolerable suffering. I needed to find the peace to let her go.

She was taken to chemotherapy in the morning and I only got to see her in the afternoon. She seemed ok afterward; however, that night she was in such intense pain that they had to sedate her with more medication. She never woke up from that deep sleep. Mum died a week after going into a coma, due to the chemo. It was a sad and difficult time for my dad to lose both of them in the same month. We all grieved in our own way. What I cherished the most was spending just over three weeks with her to tell her how much I love her and to reassure her spirit will endure.

Her death taught me about the impermanence of life and that each day of life was a precious gift. One of the greatest things that I could do to honour Mum and my brother was to appreciate life and live it to its fullest. I set my intention to cherish every moment of aliveness that my mum and brother could not. With each day that passed, I moved past the grief. In the months afterward, I continued to access consciousness in my meditations.

TRANSCENDENCE

It was clear that something in me had changed forever. It felt like an upgrade to my entire Being, a shift to the next level of consciousness. And it was a persistent state. A lifetime of soul-searching and journeying to return was replaced with a sense that I had *arrived.* Some call it enlightenment, ascension, transcendence, connection to Source consciousness, or Oneness with All that Is/God/Universe. I refer to this persistent awakened state as *transcendence*. Until now, I never had this level of contentment and peace for an extended period of time. My once-busy mind was now still and felt empty. All around my body was freedom and spaciousness.

Before my own transition, I had a similar experience about a year prior. I was just about to start my three-day healing training with about fifty other students when I noticed feeling energised as well as changes to my thinking. My mind was now very quiet and unusually still. The heavy processing fast pace of my rational mind overall was no longer there. Any thoughts remaining were slower, had a calmer quality, and didn't have the same intensity. It was as if a switch in my thoughts was turned off. *How* was this possible? I turned to the student beside me to ask her if she noticed it too; she grinned and said "absolutely!" We were both in awe and disbelief. In that moment I knew that the presence of pure consciousness itself can instantly affect our mind and state. Also, that it can affect large groups. I didn't connect the two events and had identical changes until I actually transcended. After the healing, it did not seem to persist, but after my transition, the change was lasting due to the meditations awards.

THE AWAKENED

I began to wonder if other people had experienced what I had and if it was what enlightenment felt like. I searched online to find others who had the same types of changes as I did. This led me to Deepak Chopra's book *Metahuman* on awakening human consciousness. In this book, Chopra mentioned research conducted by Dr Jeffery A. Martin at the California Institute of Integral Studies. Martin's study documents the various ways ordinary people have experienced long-term spiritual change and persistent heightened consciousness awareness and what they experienced afterward. He uses the term Fundamental Well-being to describe this long-term change to them. His research, spanning over seventeen years, categorises stages of awakening into five main levels but there are more levels beyond those, with a deepening of the effects towards level five and beyond. All of the awakened reported the following changes:

- Many experienced a persistent connection to consciousness
- A sense that the body extends further than the physical body
- A significant decrease in self-related thoughts
- Experienced inner completion and a sense that everything is okay
- A decrease in emotional intensity and being less impacted
- Able to maintain focus on the present moment and decreased past or future thinking
- Changes to the memory combined with less ability to recall the past

Next, I have provided more details about each of the changes mentioned as well as added some of my first-hand own experiences of this awakened state.

Experiencing a persistent connection to consciousness:

Before my shift, I felt separated and disconnected from the source. After my awakening, I feel permanently connected and conscious and can access even deeper levels of consciousness when I choose to. I am deeply connected to my Divine Self and feel less connected to the material world. Source consciousness feels like an overlay over my personality as well as in my daily life. I also feel that the lifelong soul-searching phase of my life is over and replaced with a sense of arrival or return.

A sense that the body extends further than the physical body:

To me, it feels as if I am no longer just a physical body, I am the field of consciousness around me. Being a part of the field is expansive and spacious. I feel energetically different, less physical, and more the energy and light of my Divine Self. It feels as if I've permanently "upgraded" my energy and made the shift to the next level of light.

A significant decrease in self-related thoughts:

All participants in the study reported a significant decrease in self-related thinking with some indicating up to an 80-95% decrease. I experienced a reduction of most thoughts, especially those relating to myself, of judgments, over-analysing, anxious thoughts as well as rumination. In addition to this, less judgment of others. The remaining thoughts are either planning/work-related or creative insight and ideas. For me, having significantly fewer thoughts and a still mind has changed my life the most.

Inner completion and a sense that everything is okay:

Some participants at certain awakened levels also experience a perpetual state of joy, peace, and love. There is a deep knowing inside me that everything will be okay, despite my life being just as busy and full as before. And with that knowledge, I don't engage in the same anxious thinking that once dominated my life.

I experience this as *not being able* to worry, I know that my higher mind doesn't need to worry, it believes in itself. I now find myself allowing life to unfold instead of trying to control or plan.

A decrease in emotional intensity and being less impacted:

I have experienced a decrease in the intensity of my emotions since Awakening. It is easier to remain neutral. It becomes easier to observe my emotions as it arises, slow my reaction and be able to detach from them more quickly afterward. This reduction in emotional intensity could also be due to thoughts having less pull. In the evenings I simply relax and move into transcendent states of peace, joy, and love with ease.

Able to maintain focus on the present moment and decrease past or future thinking:

This experience has been a wonderful state of the present moment. It feels like the timelessness of being able to observe this reality. I feel as if I no longer need to dwell on or ruminate about *myself* in the past with judgments or expectations.

Things about the past rarely pop up. It feels as if I can leave the past where it is, whilst knowing that I will recall it if it's important and when required. Since I am more present, I feel a sense of liberation from the past.

Changes to the memory and less ability to recall the immediate past:

Before the changes, there have been many instances where I've simply let things slip when I had too much on my mind. To offset changes in memory, I've had to be more conscientious in recording tasks to do and scheduling appointments immediately. I often try to tackle small tasks as soon as possible. An important distinction is that knowledge and learning are still stored in memory, and can be accessed when needed and not disappeared altogether.

A sense of oneness with the soul and universe:

The research describes the later levels as deepening and with this comes a greater sense of unity with divinity. Alongside the deep love of my Divine Self, there is a sense that Source consciousness is experiencing physical life through me.

TRANSFORMING BELIEFS

Martin concludes that despite transitioning, your conditioned way of being is still present and can take up to two years afterward to recondition most of it to adjust and up to seven years to recondition deep triggers that often result in negative reactions.

I write about Martin's research and my own experiences because often true stories can help shift your mind from possibility to reality. Whilst for some, change is a process that takes time, if you are willing to be open-minded and flexible, your mind can change quickly. The infinite part of you, the unconscious self already knows what's in the way and how you can transform, even though you may not consciously have the answer yet. Having a session with a coach can speed up the process to clear beliefs. For my own clients I would ask what their beliefs about consciousness are, how long it would take and how they believe enlightened states are achieved. Sessions often involve reframing, releasing doubts, guided meditation combined with any healing, energy transmission and light activations. After the sessions, I provide additional light transmission and an awareness practice they can do on their own.

At the time of my own transformation, I didn't have a reliable way to transcend, so I relied on my Divine Self to take me there. In addition to this, in the years leading up to this, I was led to numerous mindset training and awareness practices and that helped me change the way I think resulting in freedom from unhelpful thinking patterns and increased my well-being overall, which I detail next.

TRANSCENDING THE EGO-SELF

Transcendence didn't just happen overnight; it was the culmination of years of healing, channeling, and intuition training that began in my early 20s. Despite years of spiritual work, I realised that I still experienced a lot of self-judgment, overwhelm, stress, feeling not enough or ineffective, lacking self-trust/confidence, and limiting beliefs. I realised that to speed up my spiritual growth, I needed to do deeper inner work on my ego-self/personality and change my thinking.

With this in mind, I started taking personal development courses in hypnosis, mindfulness, emotional mastery, neuroscience, inner child, shadow work, psychology, and developmental coaching.

Ken Wilber proposes there are four stages of awakening and development. *Waking up is* the first stage of spiritual awareness and knowing who you are. *Growing up* is about taking responsibility for your behaviour and emotional maturing. *Cleaning up* is the process of recognising and changing existing patterns, conditioning or triggers in order to choose appropriate responses. Finally, *Showing up* is the last stage which relates to service to a greater cause.

Wilber's pathway was a more integrated approach to enlightenment of self, not just the spiritual practices, but the work on my emotional development and outdated patterns that kept me stuck. In addition to this, I learned developmental coaching, which helped me the most by shifting my mindset.

Coaching helped me the most by shifting my mindset. I realised that the suffering I had experienced earlier in life was psychological and showed me how I had created it. The sessions helped me shift the way I perceived the world. I viewed reality in a subjective way through my interpretation of reality. This interpretation was coloured by my beliefs, values, memories, decision, meaning-making, and thinking patterns otherwise known as perceptual filters. I realised that my unhappiness was due to the way I was constructing the story of my life. I was not accurately seeing both sides of my life and *distorting* my view of life; I was *deleting* the parts of my life that were working and okay, I was generalising that most of my life was work, obligation, and responsibility. A lot of my attention was focused on what was wrong or missing in my life, what I don't have, and what I haven't achieved instead of what was working well. I was also mean-ing-making in unhelpful ways, by putting it all together and it meant lack of fulfilment. To find acceptance that life is what it is

Undoubtedly, this inner work has helped me in so many ways to retrain my mind and optimise it to see life in a way that enhances each moment of my life.

CONCLUSION

Nowadays, I work as a spiritual teacher and coach because I am passionate about helping people who have experienced an inner calling move along their path. I help those who have awakened and want to ascend in this lifetime to make a transformational shift in their consciousness to their level of light. I share this passion by chan-neling the information from the universal mind and my Divine Self.

If you would like to know more about the ascension pathway, to be able to master energy, sacred geometry, dimensional light, be able to transform your light body, and be able to hold finer frequencies and patterns of light and consciousness, you can find out more at *consciouscentre.com*.

ABOUT LINH WHYATT

Linh is the founder of Empowered Path and Conscious Centre, a coaching and personal development training business. She comes from a creative background as a digital experience designer and creates traditional watercolour artwork. In addition to this, she has a career in finance as a property entrepreneur. She has been featured in two books, *The Book of Success* and *The Australian Property* book. Linh has trained in many holistic modalities and started a business in 2003 in London and more recently in 201o in Sydney, She is an intuitive channel, Reiki Master, Sound Healer, Reconnective healer, and Theta healer. She is also a certified NLP coach who provides one-on-one coaching, group programs, and individual light-consciousness sessions. Her mission is to help people who are awakening to Who They Really Are on their journey of connecting to Source, Transcendence, and Ascension to find inner peace, feel complete, experience inner stillness, and be. She offers transformational coaching to help clear any beliefs that may prevent you from accessing higher consciousness, clear your past programming, and be present in the now.

Websites: *www.consciouscentre.com*
www.empoweredpath.com.au
Facebook: *www.facebook.com/consciouscentre*
www.facebook.com/empoweredpathsydney

9

OLIVIA BANGERT

JOURNEY TO THE CHALLENGE

The boxes of syringes were jostled in my dresser drawer. I couldn't find the needle I was looking for. These would have to work. I squeezed my fingers between the lid and the side of a box and grabbed one. My other hand clenched a cold vial. I pulled off the cap and pushed the needle tip in. I closed one eye to get the drop in focus. It smelled like Band-Aids.

I pushed the needle into a pinch of my stomach, fast, holding it down so the liquid went in. I felt a jab of pain radiating and a pearl of blood came out. I grabbed a tissue and ripped it in half. Pushed the paper against the blood.

I didn't feel any different—I rarely did, the two years I'd been doing this. Sometimes with the perfect amount it was like caffeine and a childlike burst of energy after a nap. It crossed my mind that maybe I took too much. I was tired but wasn't going to sleep yet.

The wildfires started a few weeks ago. I sent a photo of the hot hoggy sky to Anna and Sadie when I was driving on Highway 29 by the split for Sonoma where we'd been for Anna's bachelorette. The clouds were burnt ruby red. I texted, "thank goodness bachelorette was last weekend! So smokey!!!!"

It'd been a few years since the last bachelorettes, showers, celebrations, the last bridesmaid's dresses, and coincidentally, my diagnosis. It was hard after Anna's. It still triggered feelings when I was in hiding in flowers down the aisles and wanted my own plans back. Dreams back. My own marriage back. Not the same one, but something building on all the memories and celebrations. Something real. Not the life I discovered my husband had with a bridal magazine model from Alabama a week after our honeymoon.

My dad sent a message as I was texting Anna and Sadie. "Father-daughter weekend in Shingletown still on!" I hadn't been sure because of the fires. One was still unpredictable coming down on South Lake Tahoe. We were headed into the land of the largest burning wildfire in California's history. The Dixie Fire. It was the last weekend Eddie was alive.

Day 10

I turned thirty-seven and went to Calistoga like we did when I turned thirty-six. I was with my parents this year. It wasn't real yet. It was like a Food & Wine magazine photoshoot in the desert with palm trees and turquoise pools and vineyard hills burning orange and maroon. Grace dropped off a birthday gift for me at the hostess desk. She'd been with us at my parents' house last weekend in Piedmont. It was my idea. I picked up black bottom cake from Ladyfinger's. There were palm trees on it like I asked. Those little plastic ones. Blue frosting read, "Happy Birthday Eddie." He died two days before thirty-nine. Ten days before my thirty-seven. Numbers and dates were everywhere. Numbers start to be all you have like it's still holding on.

Anna sent flowers to Piedmont and Sadie came over. I called them at my parents' house in the courtyard by the kitchen.

The news was on. The Forest Service just closed all parks in California. On the last day I talked to Eddie, South Lake Tahoe was put under mandatory evacuation. Eddie was packing and trying on his new Hawaiian shirts. One with surfboards and one with palm trees. I called him while I was dropping off my sapphire in Piedmont for the safe. He told me about his new shirts and I told him I'd call him back when I was home. His mom sent a photo of fires burning in the distance from St. Helena.

Later that night, after we hung up, the last message he sent me was about a dinner reservation on the Big Island. I was exhausted and battling low blood sugar all night, but I was happy. A new season of celebration and adventure was starting with Hawaii. Our birthdays, holidays, the wedding. It wasn't perfect but it was real. More real than I'd ever felt.

Our flight was the next morning, but we never made it.

Day 15

I couldn't read his book. He just finished writing it and I was going to read it in Hawaii. Angie with her type 1 diabetes. Buddy and his love for Angie. Angie's purple sweater, like mine with the brown buttons.

Grace wrapped a printed copy in gold wire ribbon, in gold tissue, in the pink bag, tied with the ring pouch for my birthday.

Day 20

"Owww!" I cried, from the needle. The alarm vibrations had been ringing in my ear all night. Like the night before and before. Tears triggered trembled. A few weeks ago he asked me how many units. "How many units do you think? Three?" I'd tell him how many I thought and then he'd tell me how many he thought.

I was alone. When I finally went home to my house in Oakland, it all rushed back. It felt like the week after I met my ex-husband's girlfriend by happenstance seven years earlier. The shock and change instantaneous. The day after she knocked on the door I flew home. I sat in my house, our house then, empty. Calling into work meetings: "Nope, we haven't got the wedding photos back yet, soon... yes, the Maldives were amazing. Tokyo. Singapore. The trip of a lifetime." That's the thing about betrayals in a marriage; until you decide to leave, you start living a lie.

I took in the familiar smell of my house. The fires had been bad that week and there was a subtle undertone of smoke. Stinging and burning in my eyes. Swelling and humid in my chest. Cold empty air in the room. I turned on the heater and sat on the floor.

Day 28

I looked in the brown bag of recycling in the kitchen and saw four beer cans. That's weird. I only remember drinking two. Maybe three.

I walked up the spiraling wood stairs to the roof and sat at the top with the door cracked. I took out the joint I'd rolled and sparked a flame from the lighter. Scratchy speakers singing connected to my phone. Slowly inhaling warm texture channeled between thin tissue paper. Exhaling and watching the curls catch in the wind jumping like tadpoles. I felt a bulge of excess air in a house meant for a family and wanted to escape out the roof door with it.

My blood sugar alarm was going off. I lay down on the top step and closed my eyes. My head felt heavy. I opened one eye and tapped the screen to see the number. It was 285 and arrows going up. I didn't want to deal with it. I let the smoke curls grip tight inside and take me to my dreams.

I woke up to the alarm again a few hours later. Over 300 now. I stared at the roof door, still cracked, still laying on my back. I rolled over slowly and sat up.

"I should've been a cowboy; I should've learned to rope and ride. Wearin' my six-shooter, ridin' my pony on a cattle drive..." the lyrics twirled up the stairs from the scratchy speakers.

I slid on my butt down the stairs, one at a time. I turned to the left at the bottom of the stairs to the guest room and stood up. There were a few needles on top of the dresser. I grabbed one.

Twist, pull, poke, click, stab, squeeze. Blood again.

The alarm went off and I threw it across the room. I sat down on the bed and stared at the wall—a hairline crack running from the ceiling behind the dresser mirror. My head felt heavy again. I laid back on a pillow. I looked up at the ceiling. I had no idea about time.

A spider crawling on the ceiling caught my hazy gaze. I watched it. Counting its legs. It crossed over a brownish-red spec that stood out against the white paint of the ceiling. Then another spec. A cluster of tiny drops. I blinked and wrinkled my nose to clear my eyes into focus. The cluster was concentrated in a small circle like it was blown through the air. It looked like a shotgun splatter. Straight up on the ceiling. What the hell is that? Seriously. What is it and how did blood get in that pattern on my ceiling.

Day 32

I landed in Boston by myself in the morning on a red eye. Took a taxi to the hotel. Grace called to say she saw a reminder on Eddie's phone about the ferry and Airbnb reservation in Nantucket. Eddie wanted to show me where he spent a summer with his dad writing and admiring authors like Hemingway and Jack London. It was a memory of a time when his dad did love him, did want his family, did want to be a dad.

But the only part of our itinerary I'd keep was the Boston hotel. They let me check in early for a fee and I collapsed on the white duvet over white sheets.

I stared at the white towel hanging by the bathroom. I opened my phone, my photos; the selfie I sent my mom in the airport and a screenshot of an e.e. Cummings poem about Buffalo Bill's defunct.

I let the tears swell and roll from the inside of my eyes down over my nose to the side of my cheek, pioneering the fastest trail, eventually gathering into my ear and on the top of the covers. I blinked and listened to piano chords curling out of my phone.

Two days later I'd take the bus north to New Hampshire to meet my sister in her new house and my parents who planned the trip months ago.

Day 35

My mom went with me to Anna's wedding in New York. We drove south from the house they rented in Vermont. Leaves falling were the color of wildfires and wine. The estate was perched on a hill above the Hudson River. I met Anna in her bridal suite early in the morning. A pregnant photographer was testing the light with practice shots. Downstairs, the narrow ballroom was set up with two long banquet tables reminding me of Lina's wedding dinner at Blenheim Palace.

Sadie held my hand during the ceremony. That night the room filled with Irish music and dancing. Celebration. Piano and guitar. I left early; hugging Amelia and her husband goodbye on the way out. All I could feel was a cannonball in the lower corners of my eyes and stomach.

Day 49

I hadn't been to San Francisco in months and there was a work happy hour. I decided to take Uber. I grabbed a Drake's bottle from one of the ice bins on my way to the roof. Trays of hot dogs in striped paper and buckets of popcorn lined up. Crowds of youngsters. Most I didn't know. I walked over to a few partners I knew. They were talking about baseball and I tried to listen but wasn't hearing a word. I hugged a coworker I knew who came up to us with her oversized belly. "Congratulations," I said, "when's your due date?"

I grabbed a bottle opener next to spilled popcorn. I was getting tired already. It felt like old times when I had to wear my shell. I saw Carolina and remembered when we were at the Manager retreat in Sonoma after I got back from the Maldives. We had egg white omelets and it was on the tip of my tongue to tell her what was going on. I rehearsed it in my head. I deserve to tell the story. Say what's going on.

After a minute of catching up with her and the small talk, I said goodbye. Blain caught me as I was walking out and asked about Eddie. I told him Eddie died.

Day 50

I woke up to a muffled beeping noise. I was in my house. My tee shirt was wet. My hands were tingling. I was on my side. My eyelids fluttered open and closed. I tried to focus towards the light coming from the guest room. I smelled beer and peanut butter. The beeping again, a little louder. My body felt heavy and empty. Beads of sweat were moving down my forehead. I became aware there were only a few minutes. My alarm was usually on the nightstand but the only thing I saw was a beer can, green with yellow letters I couldn't read in the dark. I started to feel tingling in my tongue and the roof of my mouth.

The beeping again, louder and faster, coming from my closet. I got myself to sit up and felt tingling spread over my cheeks and neck. I heard the owl hooting from behind the house. That's weird. I hadn't heard it for months. I paused, anticipating. It was quiet otherwise like it always was in the house.

What if I did nothing? What if I laid back on the pillow like I wanted. The weight. Familiar and unwelcome, I named her in my grief journaling class: Cannabella. Like divorce pending roof leaking lawyers calling papers stacking; she was with me then. Smiling in rhinestone hair and makeup.

She'd sit on top of me and unpack a backpack each night after work when I arrived. She'd take out the heavy old pinball machines and set them on my chest. I'd stare into the depths of their lights and sounds and time would pass through me like clouds.

Like laying in an ICU bed alone while everyone is building and the only thing unraveling chronically faster than relationships and truth is health.

I got myself to stand up. My robe was in a heap on the floor. The beeping again. I reached into the robe pocket and felt it. It was lit up and showed 32 in red with the arrows going down. I bobbled down the stairs to the kitchen and a wave of ravishing took over me. Hunger in my brain, heart, blood. A contracting that was squeezing me and I'd be in a puddle any minute.

Day 55

I cracked open a beer and put it next to my laptop out of view of the camera. The weight again. I could avoid it bits at a time, but after work, the dark ascended. Different each day, heavier, pushing, holding, blocking, controlling. I sat in my dining room chair with my feet flat in front of me. The meeting started and I opened my sketchbook to a fresh page. My new pens were in a gold jar. It was quiet. I went off-camera here and there to drink the beer. I wasn't supposed to be drinking on class day but shit who can handle this. It's a group yes but really it's just me. Hope dripping back down into stalactites, frozen.

I picked up the blue pen. Sapphire blue. A horse with long eyelashes. Big blue ponds reflecting back to each other. Nose to nose. Patterns and emotions and I pulled the pen down the page bringing to life the horse's nostrils and hair. Two front legs each different. One with little windows. Love swelling and lifting and the dam broke. It felt like it would drain dry but it never did.

Day 60

I dialed the number. Held my breath. The palms of my hands were wet and my tongue was stuck to the roof of my mouth. I rambled a few introductory words and hit mute to force myself to pause. A guy with a deep voice asked for the name. "One minute, pulling it up, the report just came back," he said. It wasn't signed off yet; the doctor still needed to make the final determination, but it was back. He continued like he was reading a grocery list. I had no idea what I was hearing; sounding out the words as I rushed to grab a pen and write them all down on the back of a Target receipt.

I stared out the window at brown birds jumping on a tree limb. I felt a cold sensation form in my stomach. An electric coil contracting. Let's not mix up matters of the heart with stone-cold facts.

II.

It started with making a decision. To turn inward. Listen to the quiet voice wanting to be heard.

It's not going to get louder. You have to get quiet inside yourself to hear. It's always there and always the truth. I was numbing and distracting and protecting myself from moments I'd have to sit alone in pain. Painful feelings popping from every pin prick.

These painful moments exist. When we numb and protect ourselves from feelings like isolation, shame and disconnection we also numb the voices of hope, curiosity in the unknown, and love.

Maybe my diabetes was saving me because the only thing I could hear was that damn alarm. I wanted to shut it up. There was only one way to quiet it. The only structure I could grasp then was the thirty-day challenge. It was January already and I had to make a decision. Would I do the challenge again this year on my own?

I already knew how to do it. It was one of few things I felt connected to. I wanted hope back. Love back. Curiosity in the unknown back.

My awakening started with 30 days: the salad challenge. I did it the year before with Eddie. Going to the store and chopping and tossing and roasting on my own was exhausting. As Day 1 turned into Day 10 an old spark was morphing inside me. My energy was growing. I was doing it for myself. Choosing myself. Creating for myself. I'd never done that before with basic self care like healthy cooking. A ritual too small to mess up.

I created every day; something just for me. I started to hear my intuition get louder. With better health I could start listening. My determination was coming back. Motivation to honor all that had happened.

These things didn't happen to me; they happened for me. Like wildfires, now they were going to happen through me.

By the end of the thirty days I needed less insulin, used fewer needles, and had mental clarity. Energy and creativity that would build. I lost weight and looked healthier. I was creating something new and trusting I could complete a promise to myself.

As January rolled into February, Russia invaded Ukraine. Molotov cocktails and petrol bombs. That grandma shoving flower seeds into a Russian soldier's pocket as he was scurrying her along.

I didn't know it, but the salad challenge was setting me up for a deeper challenge. One I'd hidden from my whole life. I knew what I needed to do. It was hard and I couldn't do this one on my own. I needed help.

I sat on the floor and took out an envelope listing each day as it came:

Day 1: February 23, morning [x], evening [x]
Day 2: February 24, morning [x], evening [x]
Day 3: February 25, morning [x], evening [ ]

The second week was hell. When my blood sugar alarm went off in the middle of the night I threw it across the room and screamed so loud the neighbors knocked on the door. I picked up the potted plant and threw it, the pot shattering. Dirt everywhere. Feelings coming out. Really coming out. All the anger I'd pushed down coming out. When you cut out distractions the reward system is re-wiring; nothing left to numb the feelings down.

Then the dreams started. Almost every night. I had to journal them they were so vivid.

It was uncomfortable to tell people I wasn't drinking. But I did. I stuck to it. I started connecting to people who understood. I started writing again. I listened. And I started to attract better. I started to feel relaxed in my dreams.

I knew something special was happening as I was swinging my legs on the back of a white pickup truck one evening, on a picnic blanket—a surprise salad challenge laid out in front of me—sipping Spindrifts and water from coconuts.

I looked out over the city lights and the bridges and the skyscrapers. I was happy. I was healthy. I trusted and accepted.

Acceptance. Not wishing it happened differently. And most importantly bloom again.

You created that. You can do it again. And again.

ABOUT OLIVIA BANGERT

Olivia is a health coach and a healthcare consultant for top U.S. hospitals. She was inspired to become a coach when she had to lead herself through an unexpected type 1 diabetes diagnosis in 2019. After overcoming years of struggling with mindset and health challenges without a diagnosis from her clinical support team until she landed in the ICU, she knew she could help others get faster results to succeed in their journey using her experience built within healthcare, diabetes, thriving after big life changes, and being her own entrepreneur for financial success. Olivia is certified by the International Coaching Federation (ICF) as a Life Coach. She earned certification in Innovation and Entrepreneurship from Stanford University in 2020 and believes everyone is an entrepreneur with their health journey. She built her career in consulting and is currently a director for a leading healthcare revenue management firm. She has spent over a decade fighting health insurance companies for accurate reimbursement for care to patients with diabetes and other health conditions. Her healthcare reimbursement expertise is something she offers to clients who need additional help navigating the healthcare system.

Websites: *www.typeonecoach.com*
www.oliveblooms.com
LinkedIn: *www.linkedin.com/in/oliviab*
Instagram: *www.instagram.com/typeonecoach*

10

SAFEERA KHOLVADIA

*E*veryone has an untold story, a broken fragment of their past, buried in the shadows of memory. Some tales are never meant to be hidden because they have the power to shape the decisions of future generations. My life has been one of such tales—a tale of how I conquered the weaknesses of my past, using my experiences as a chisel to chip away at a creative block of healing. By writing here, I get to taste life twice, in the moment and in retrospection.

My story took a decisive turn on a busy Saturday night. It was my first year in residency as a newly qualified medical doctor. I was thrown into the deep end of our public hospital surgical emergency department and was put in charge of seeing to and managing different emergencies:

Gunshot wounds
Check

Stab wounds
Check

Axe lodged in skull

CHECK

Motor Vehicle Accident on a Gurney
CHECK, CHECK

Overdose
CHECK

RESUSCITATION
CHECK, CHECK, CHECK

Don't get attached
Check

No feelings attached
Check

Numb the empathy
Check

"Patients=
Can't save them all."
CHECK, CHECK, CHECK, CHECK

Traumatized
CHECK

Trauma inside
CHECK

After endless resuscitations, though, I was startlingly calm.

Absolutely unfazed, triaging as they came along. Without flinching, I carried out my practice methodically, and it felt so mechanical. It was like I was trapped and had no clue I was in a trance.

Trauma and the creative process are age-old bedfellows. I had no way to fully cope with what I was doing. In all my years of study, no one lecture covered emotional, collective, or ancestral trauma. We practiced Response Medicine; problem-solve actions.

My detached education style and detached personal history were so ingrained in me for years, making me more mechanical and more efficient.

Fighting the fretful wakefulness of insomnia is rarely fun, but it turned into my most mystic creative tool.

Sometimes, after a somewhat thirty-six-hour shift, the aftermath of terror would come caving in. I can recall taking long walks alone along the quiet and peaceful hospital corridors with the sound of occasional beeps from machines and monitors echoing in the silence. I would find myself checking in on a 600g premature baby, lost in my thoughts. Some days, I would find myself sitting in the neonatal ward and stroking the little baby's hand-tracing the map of blue veins beneath the paper-thin skin, and I felt the strange peace of doing nothing, yet, doing so much.

It was always in these moments of reflection and sinking deep into the stillness of my thoughts that I began to ask myself some questions. Where did my spark go? How had I lost myself? "I'm dying to be me," I would whisper to it, knowing I wouldn't get a response from her. Tangible grief comes up when the thick layer of what's holding your identity together comes up for dusting and clearing.

My mechanical and sterile practices were felt in my daily life. I started life as a butterfly with freedom and flexibility and ended up in a rigid cocoon. It was during one of my corridor thoughts in the hospitals I figured out that I had traded my black superhero cape (from my imagination) for a white lab coat.

I was conflicted because medicine was my bedrock. Before the world told me who to be, who was I? The only world I knew—MEDI-CINE, the so-called opium of the intellectuals. I've always felt like my most multi-dimensional place, though, was a library, and that significantly shaped my view of life.

I can still remember my first book ever. I can still see it. The graphic, the design... It was called the "Ugg-ly-duck-leeng." This was the way I spelled it—I always had trouble spelling it out at that little age. I recall seeing these gigantic words and pop-out pictures. I was in boarding school, and I could not mask the feeling of excitement painted all over my face. The tides, however, soon began to turn when I brought it home, and an aunt looked at me and huffed in disgust.

"Out of all the books in the library, why would you choose this one?" were her words.

I was so excited to read it. I didn't sense anything wrong with the book—the book smelt of the triumph and adventure of a duckling. Besides, it was the first book I ever read by myself! The Ugly Duckling.

Somehow, that became a moment. One of many to come. Those moments when the world sat me down and told me to be quiet. They pointed at my cages and showed me the feelings I was allowed to express. An endless list of rules and doctrines. A new truth that shrouded my innocent mind with a myriad of unanswered questions about the confusing balance between right and wrong.

They would tell me, "This is how a girl should act...," "This is the body you must strive for...," "These are the things you should believe...," "These are the people you can love..." "These are the people you should fear...," "These are the books you can read...," "This is the kind of life you are meant to desire..."

They would tell me to keep myself fitting in, stating that although I would be uncomfortable at first, it would eventually become a norm, and I would forget that I was caged.

The realization was exhausting, but it soon began to shape my mind. I began to internalize my formal taming. I wanted to be a 'good girl.' I had reached the stage when children start to hide who they indeed are to become what the world expects them to be. So I tried to control myself. I chose a personality, a body of faith, and a sexuality so tiny and claustrophobic. I had to hold my breath to fit myself inside.

I was restless and frustrated, and I soon became very ill. My heart was constantly troubled by all the confusion, and I struggled with severe migraines, followed up shortly with a diagnosis of a heart conduction defect.

As I gained knowledge, I held on to my goal of being a good girl, but this pattern created someone else. A naive young woman was soon birthed. I was saying yes even when my heart screamed NO! It was my powerplay as I grew up, and some traumas survived as residues, some of them all the more virulent because borders no longer hemmed them in. It was at this point that I refused to comply. I indulged my hunger and hid my mother wounds, menstruation wounds, sister wounds, womb wounds, and my constant confrontation with life and death situations. Then, I would drape myself over the toilet and purge from the severe build-up of tension because a 'good girl' must make herself very small and thin to fit inside her cages.

My short adolescent life was a long and endless suicide. Soon, the awkward melancholy got into my tone. My flicker was always inside me, smoldering, but I sure as hell felt gone for a long while. My childhood smallness soon morphed into prescription painkiller addictions, causing me to stay numb for years. I admit that I could always hear that still voice that I had buried beneath decades of numbing and social conditioning. It was always there, whispering calmly within me. After so many years of playing contortionist, writhing, bending, curving, convoluting, and knotting myself to fit inside some stranger's idea of love, I finally had a turning point at an event ironically called TURNING POiNT. It was my battle cry and rejoicing all at once. I felt alive. I tasted freedom in the jolt, and I wanted more.

I realized how my one eye is always following the sacred and ancient patterns of the universe, and the idea of multiple universes, multiple realities, beyond the five senses was a disturbing discovery in our established academia.

I looked hard at all my ships—kinship, friendship, relationships, work, and sexuality. I slowly built a new identity, a sober faith, a new purpose, a new family, a kindled marriage, a new worldview lens, and a new sense by design instead of default from my imagination. Instead of my indoctrination, it was the reactivation of my dormant powerful feminine self and the merging of my powerful, holding masculine self. I began to cultivate a love for myself that was custom-made by me.

Pregnancy was probably the field in which I began to remember my wild days. I already had three beautiful children, and at what seemed like my lowest point with postpartum depression, failing relationships, and failing businesses, I finally asked myself that golden question. That question of AM I READY TO TRADE EXPECTATIONS FOR ACCEPTANCE?

This was my galvanizing wake-up call about what is possible at a soul level. It was a profoundly personal, eye-opening, wise, unapologetic, ferocious, and deeply challenging step.

I asked myself how much of this was my idea. Did I truly want any of this? Or was it what I was conditioned to want? Which of the beliefs of my creation were programmed into me? How much of who I've become is inherent in me, and how much was just inherited? How much of my personality was a product of negotiating with fear of how I should behave, look, and speak?

Only I know the ego deconstruction that I've gone through; I would say that it has been hard-winning work, a journey of an everyday "YES." And oh so sacred to my heart. At first, it seemed like an impossible mountain to climb, but over time, I found myself walking away from my cages. When I stepped out and declared, "HERE I AM," it felt like receiving an intravenous drip and a fist-pumping adrenalized rightness. The ecstasy was beyond words; although it is a continuous process, I understand myself better now.

It involves a FREE FALL of a significant ego surrender to withdraw from and have the luxury to WITHDRAW TO, as I pulled my overextended, misplaced, creative energy into my core.

None of these exciting activities was a short antidote to the poison of irrationality, inseparable from human interactions but fatal to them if granted a life of its own. Being human isn't in separate and independent activities but in the connection between ourselves.

My Awakened Feminine has hundreds of voices in my journey and hundreds more to come, I suspect. In that sense, there is no such thing as an individual voice. There is only personal responsibility; some of these are within their own borders. If we can't remember them all, we should at least have some idea of what we have forgotten. For a while, I wished to go along without remembering and gain all the advantages of 'traveling light.' Still, a deep instinct not very different from love reminds me that efficiency would be bought at the cost of emptiness. These are the words that came from within. I have re-emerged. I have rearranged my cellular makeup. Reborn as a different person. My Awakened feminine is an anthem for me, and I desire it to become an anthem for other women too.

Pain is not tragic. Pain is magic. Suffering is tragic. As an Awakened Feminine Leader, I only take orders from my own sense of knowing. Fortunately, I see it as a gift. My childhood set the stage for motherhood and martyrdom. I had to learn the lesson well—a lesson echoed in these words:

"There comes the point where we need to stop just pulling people out of the river. We need to go upstream and find out why they are falling in." - Desmond Tutu

We are storied beings through and through.

We and the Universe are inseparable partners in a timeless embrace, and we are collaboratively dreaming up the Universe while the Universe is simultaneously dreaming us up!

Now, I recognize that I needed science to show me my poetry, and I am glad I found it. All we need to do is to be ourselves. As a child, I was this living technology that felt what it needed to handle, and I followed my gut. I planned only from my imagination and became wild until I was tamed by shame.

Today, as I glance through the pages of one of my favorite books, Nassim Taleb's "The Black Swan," I realize there are no coincidences!

Go figure, the story of the highly improbable from THE UGLY DUCKLING TO THE BLACK SWAN. As I reminisce on the past and all the accumulated experience effect, I can say they are salutary, perhaps even if solitary.

It's at times like this that I giggle and think: when the question was asked to the long line of souls waiting: "Who wants to go to Earth school?" I was right there, front and center saying ME! ME! ME!

I am a missioned soul and here to master self-mastery and mirror that inspiration to every being I come into contact with, with an unapologetic, raw, wild, and innocent primal LOVE.

I am a Bridge between science and spirituality, between Form and Formless, where Mind and Matter merge, where they come together, and all opposites come to a resolution by discovering the interconnectivity and oneness of all. It's all about the principle of *connessione*, meaning connection. I am here as a receptacle to the new incoming energies and to support various people from all over the world who are beginning to experience new joy as they merge with the new positive energies of the millennium.

It doesn't matter if your beginning film looks like an unedited home video. At the heart of the anorexia of creative avoidance is the denial of process. The magic lies not in the done but in DOING. Sure, it's ingrained that we need to go out often and shake a few trees to make things happen. Sometimes we find ourselves painting with scissors; I can't deny that shaking a few trees to make things happen is true. In fact, it is necessary. Sometimes I've shaken a tree thinking apples would fall out, but I got oranges instead. Still so grateful for the ABUNDANCE!

My story is not only about synchronicity but about the right dependence on the universe as a source.

My story serves as a reminder that THERE IS SUCH A MEDICINE IN BEING A WOMAN.

It's taken me a lifetime—perhaps lifetimes—to meet a part of me that's so deeply connected to my femininity.

My message here is BOLD: step into the deep waters. It gets to be exciting, fearful, unforgettable, and delicious.

Experience all of you in full measure! If you want to cry, cry fully! If you're laughing, laugh fully! If you experience grief, grieve fully! If you're excited, melt into the excitement FULLY! Let all that you are and all that you feel pass through you and MOVE you.

NO HALF MEASURES, NO LUKEWARM LIVING…fully experience the hot, the pleasure, the sensual, the fear, the excitement. Claim the events of your life to MAKE YOURSELF YOURS. Don't try to figure it out.

Simply begin with the silence, feel the texture of the distance, and see the clear, bright light that has come from so far away. I may have had a little pedestrian formula to get here, but it harnessed mind and body dexterity.

Today I offer the most rudimentary nutrient: ENCOURAGEMENT via this original poem:

I AM Perfectly Me:

To be a child again
Running through unknown worlds
with a lens of innocence
Spray-painted in yellows and greens
Only blues seen here
are the ones plastered
in rarely cloudy skies
And even when the puffy whites do appear
they shapeshift into clear images
that tell stories of lions, tigers, and bears
without a single care in mind
All things were possible until bedtime
Then that meant fighting the inevitable...
REST!
Playtime inside and outside was the absolute best when imagi-
*   nation led the way*
I miss those days
when everything made sense–
a rhyme and reason
for every season and situation
Monsters turned into kind friends
Parents had eyes in the back of their heads
and could do anything

Like make a bad day good
Or turn should, could, would's,
into absolutely's!

Decades later, my lost curiosity
captured perfectly in my children's eyes–
their innocence morphed
into the same mysterious things mine did
way back when rainbows drifted casually above our heads—
they weren't doing that for me anymore,
instead, I was only seeing rainbows when it poured, and
somehow all my courage and emotions were trapped in
faded childhood memories
My divine portal closed shut
I masked up and didn't see myself as worthy
Sleepwalking through life became my virtue
until I felt the consciousness jolt me
into the awakened revolution

Then false resolutions came to me in insecurities. Questions
Like: Why am I here? and do I even matter? crossed my
mind daily
wondering if my life meant anything to anyone else but
myself...Hard to know for sure
when everyone is so closed off
in their own heads, wondering the same thing
Went from Originality to conformity
From Creativity to inactivity
Brightness to grey years to an eventual blackout, nothing but
darkness and misery
Then the spirit above hugged me so tight I had no choice but to
see the light again,
To breathe again
To heal again
To fly again

as the imperfect, perfect me
Negativity, clown thoughts scattered
Joy and positivity enveloping
the message I was hiding all along
"I WAS HERE, AND I DO MATTER"

New life lessons won't just sit idle
I will take them and pass them to any child or lack-lustered
    adult who needs to hear it
Reminding us all
that we may fall
But we have to get back up,
braving the fierce colds each time
prepared to live our predestined lives
vibrating the energy of survivors
who won't quit even when the going gets tough because deep
    inside, our divine being
shows us through every sense
exactly how WE ARE MORE THAN ENOUGH.

You are perfectly you, and you matter. So, what will you choose to do with your life on your terms? I choose to be me, all of me, as a storyteller, healer, lover, creator, connector, and so much more. My embryonic endeavor is to help you undivide yourself. *I'm a born story-teller, and that may be why if I was left to choose my own label, I would choose none...*

On graduating from medical school, we all took the Hippocratic Oath. I was a baby artist urged to think like a baby doctor. But now I've evolved from that baby doctor, from the infancy of Wounded Healer to living and acting in my mature Awakened Feminine. So with my hand on my heart, I retake my Oath and declare:

Commitment to Self Mastery:

Check

Integrity in every thought and Action:
CHECK CHECK

Humility in manner:
Check

Compassion with my journey:
Check

Honouring my personal story:
Check

LOVE at my core:
CHECK, CHECK, CHECK, CHECK

Divine service:
Check

Unattached Passion:
Check

Honour my sacred eye:
CHECK

Render myself NOT JUST WHOLE BUT HOLY:
CHECK

Be the messenger:
CHECK, CHECK, CHECK, CHECK, CHECK!

Remember, the entirety of the healing journey starts and ends with you.

ABOUT SAFEERA KHOLVADIA

Dr Safeera Kholvadia is the founder of Dr Safeera Kholvadia Global. She is a mother of three beautiful children, a medical doctor, a speaker, and a creative who loves travel and novel experience. She's passionate about the mastery of our human embodiment, the weaving of matter, and human whole-ing, as we anchor new ways of being so that we can lead a New Era for humanity and our communities. Incorporating frequency technology, multidimensional understanding, ancient alchemy and the wisdom of our bodies in matter and transcended form, she invites and supports a whole new embodiment for her clients and humanity.

She's here as a bridge between Physical and Metaphysical, Mind and Matter and helps cultivate harmony and unity on a Micro-Cellular Individual Level and a Macro-Multidimensional Societal Level. She invites us to open to allowing the highest timeline frequencies to work through us, as we become ambassadors for embodying Unity Consciousness Come and is here to pass on the MEDICINE OF BEING A WOMAN.

Safeera Kholvadia Global:
www.drsafeerakholvadiaglobal.com
Dr Safeera Kholvadia:
info@drsafeerakholvadiaglobal.com
Instagram: *www.instagram.com/Safeera_Kholvadia*

11

SARAH ASHLEY WHEELER

ou, my darling, are so powerful. I know this because you manifested this book into your world. It was you that was meant to read these words, and I'm so happy that our paths crossed in this lifetime. Let my words activate you and remind you that you are the awakened feminine.

People know me as the Energy Queen online, but what you don't know about me is how I grew up in the world and what I went through to even be on this Earth. I was born four months premature. I weighed 1 lb 5oz, and I had a twin that did not survive. From the beginning, I felt like I wasn't meant to be here. Since I was three years old, I knew I could see and feel energy. I saw guides and angels in my room and had many tea parties with them! My family would always tell me "you are special; you are meant to be here," which was confusing to me. Internally and externally, I felt misplaced. I felt like I just didn't belong. I felt like school was hard, and I didn't get it. I didn't understand why everyone else got it and I did not. Eight years ago, I looked into the mirror and said to myself, "Sarah Ashley, you have searched your whole life to find this person in the mirror, it's time that I know you more than anyone else knows you." And that's where my journey began.

Living a life feeling like I didn't have a place while looking around at other people taking up space in this world... There was always a pressure on my heart like, "What are you doing here, Sarah?" And my mom would always tell me, "You're here for a reason," over and over. And I think because she said that so much, I had to search to figure out why I was here and why my twin didn't survive.

Today I serve women around the world who feel like I felt, who know that there is a power inside of them but feel like they don't know how to tap into it. Women who feel not recognized by themselves and have not been taking up space in this world.

The frequency shift goes something like this: "Wait a minute. You mean to tell me that I am who I say that I am when I've been searching for the world to validate me?" *Yes.*

In the following words, you will see how I went from searching for meaning to activating that meaning inside of myself. You will see the power vibe boosters I say to myself daily. Today is the day you reclaim who you are here to be and what now gets to occur in your life. We are going to wake it up and shake it up and have your frequency shifted so much you become magnetic to miracles. When we come back into alignment with who we are, our frequency shifts—it moves, it lights up and you become the beacon of the light you are here to be.

What if everything that has happened to you and to me was actually so that our spirit could experience that frequency?

What if we were always meant to remember how to rise above and lift ourselves to where we know we are meant to be?

If you are experiencing a life that you're not happy with right now, what if that is your spirit saying "I'm here to simply understand this frequency so that I can remember how to shift it." I truly believe that everything I've experienced was so that I could simply just understand it but not actually stay in it. This wouldn't be an Energy Queen chapter if we didn't move energy, so let's do some energy hacking right now and light up your world so you can light up the world around you.

I want you to soak up this phrase and place your hand on your heart and tell your soul, "You Are The One." *The one* who can change her energy. *The one* who can change her story around money. *The one* who can change her life. *The one* who is here to be one of the greats in this lifetime simply because you are. *The one* who can change her mind at any moment at any time.

Today you will turn up the volume on the spark inside of your soul and let it shine brightly.

What I had to remember was in a world where people are searching for meaning but that meaning has always and forever been inside your being. You are the meaning. Your soul is the reason you are here. You have a God spark and today we tell that spark to light up and always shine. The search for all the reasons you want to understand *why* you went through what you did, ends now.

You know why, just like I knew why. My spirit wanted to understand frequencies no matter how painful it was so that I could shift them. The power has always been in my hands just as much as yours. Let's activate this now.

Let's connect to your soul and do some soul talking so that you can connect to your power.

I want you to repeat after me:

1. *Soul, show me how powerful you are by sending me a frequency so I can feel you now.*
2. *Drop me into observation to feel it.*
3. *When you feel It, say I feel you, Soul.*

1. *Soul, show me how powerful you are by bringing clarity to my mind right now so I can feel it.*
2. *Drop me into observation to feel it.*

Notice what you feel by talking to your soul and her responding back to you!

Didn't feel anything yet? Let's shake it up!

Repeat after me:

1. *Soul, I am afraid to feel energy and I'm feeling that fear right now and letting it go.*
2. Say this three times and repeat the above soul statement.

I bet you're now feeling tingles in your hands and the sensations that are having you thinking "Omgosh," "What On Earth," "Whoa I felt my soul."

Honor it. Embrace it. Told you we are shaking things up!

Now let's activate your power by connecting even more to your soul.

Repeat after me:

1. I want you to acknowledge the power coming into your body right now.

Notice how you feel saying that. Notice if you took a deep breath. When you feel it say "**YES** I feel it."

Repeat after me:

1. I want you to acknowledge all the love that you have for all of your selves right now.
2. I want you to acknowledge how it feels to love yourself and pour into yourself right now.
3. I want you to acknowledge how good that feels to say that to yourself.

Notice if you began to smile, this is because your being is doing what you tell it to.

When we say "I acknowledge," we are connecting to your spirit to come in and fill your request.

I love to go on acknowledging vibe boosters and the more I do this daily, the more power I access within myself.

How to create a frequency vibe booster.

The most important thing here is that you record what you want to step into within yourself and play this back every single day.

Things I say to myself are:

I love how amazing you are, Sarah Ashley. I love that something amazing is getting ready to happen to you today. I love that you are acknowledging your power and I love that you take up space in the world. I love how people treat you and I love how easy it is to attract new friends into your life.

When I record with my voice and play it back the power I feel inside is electrifying.

I encourage you to come back to this chapter whenever you are ready to shift your frequency and remember your power. I challenge you to create your own frequency vibe booster and listen for twenty-one days and let me know how your life shifted.

I love you and thank you for manifesting this chapter in your life. It has been an honor to share my story with you.

ABOUT SARAH ASHLEY WHEELER

Sarah Ashley, also known as the Energy Queen in the world. Her transformational way of shifting energy in people's lives has brought her into being known as the Energy Queen. She supports spiritual entrepreneurs in turning up their powers and knowing how to connect to their inner guidance so they can attract the highest calling of life and soul- mate clients.

Website: www.sarahashleywheeler.com
Email: Sarahashleywheeler@gmail.com
Facebook: www.facebook.com/sarahashleyvisionarymentor
5 Day Manifestation Challenge:
www.sarah-ashley-wheeler-126b.mykajabi.com/offers/T3V-
moEV9/checkout

12

WENDY CORNER

"This really is the first day of the rest of my life!" Those twelve words are pregnant with emotion... yet I felt nothing.

*M*y story is about feeling ALL the feels and **acknowledging them.**

The year was 2009. In my professional life, I was a very experienced Speech Pathologist who could and did advocate, sometimes fiercely, for my clients (adults with intellectual disabilities with/without autism).

I had NO problem standing up for and helping people find their voice... with a passion!

I DID have a problem standing up for myself in personal relationships.

Everyone else's voice mattered.

Mine didn't.

That was the internal script I was running and had been since I was two.

At that point in my life, I was totally clueless that this was the case.

All I knew was that I hated confrontation when it came to me. I hated upsetting people and always wanted to keep on the right side of everyone.

What happened when I was two to create this internal script?

Where did this deeply buried story I told myself come from?

The one that unconsciously shaped my life choices…?

I required surgery on my finger, which meant a stay in hospital.

Back in the 1960s parents weren't allowed to stay with their children, so my earliest memory is of the double doors closing with me on one side screaming for my Mam on the other.

She didn't come for me.

My two-year-old logic made the decision: that means my voice doesn't matter.

I also made the decision that my feelings didn't matter especially as through my childhood I was conditioned (as many of us are) to not express negative feelings and tone down the exuberant ones too!

I had an excellent role model in my Mam who kept such a lid on her emotions: ever the strong epitome of the British stiff upper lip!

So now you know the foundations, the conditioning, that resulted in me not allowing myself to feel the feels, let me get back to *that* day…

It's August 3rd, 2009, and my first day back to work after two weeks off hosting my parents for their annual holiday to Speyside, Scotland and celebrating our twentieth wedding anniversary. My routine was to phone my husband on the way home to debrief the day so that when I arrived home it was "together" time. He had been retired due to his mental ill-health.

Except today he didn't answer when I called him. I left it for a bit, and I tried again. Still no answer. So I thought about our last conversation which had been about favourite CDs for a "guess who from the album cover" team-building exercise coming up at work. I started singing one of the tracks:— – the Pie Jesu from Faure's Requiem. A beautiful ethereal piece. Except the closer I got to home, the more foreboding I felt.

I couldn't shake the feeling.

I crept in the front door, suspecting Geoff may have been taking a nap. I heard noises from the office upstairs so I popped my head around the door and, whilst the computer was on, I could see his head slumped forward in the chair.

Rather than startle him (he was constantly anxious) I walked round to face him.

That was when I saw a colour combo I never want to see again!

His arms hung limply by his sides.

His face, torso, and shoulders were a pale straw-yellow colour.

His forearms and hands were purple and mottled where the blood had drained.

He had been dead a couple of hours.

And that's when I blurted out that famous twelve-word phrase.

"This really *is* the first day of the rest of my life!"

I was numb.

I was in shock.

At forty-two, I was a widow!

At this point, I was incapable of feeling anything.

I had things to do, people to contact...

I called for an ambulance and so began the deluge of people calling round:

Ambulance crew, Neighbours, Doctor, Police, Undertakers.

Time stood still!

I felt nothing!

I phoned my parents. Mam answered.

Dissociated from any feeling I asked her if she was sitting down.

"I don't know how else to say this... Geoff is dead!"

Equally dispassionately I phoned the office and left a message on the ansaphone:

"Hi guys, it's Wendy. I won't be in tomorrow or for the foreseeable. Geoff's dead."

Over the next twenty-four hours, as news got out, my Mam got the next train to be with me, flowers started arriving...

Feeling began to seep back in.

Shock was wearing off.

The tears began to flow.

Sadness, Loneliness, Anger, Relief... say what?

Relief?

Followed swiftly by Guilt!

I had to make the mental shift from being wife and carer (a role Geoff vehemently denied, I may add!) to losing both those labels and suddenly being a widow and living alone for the first time in my life.

I had grown up in a middle-class family with two parents and my older brother. I left home to go to University and lived in Halls or shared houses until my first job when I lived in a Nurses home until I was married and

Here I am, now facing living solo.

How did that feel?

I had no idea!

Lonely? I guess so!

Sad? That came in waves, and I certainly contributed to the fortunes of Kleenex for a few weeks!!

Yet the tears weren't all about sadness and loneliness.

As I had those practical tasks to do... find paperwork, sort finances etc (these had been his responsibility!) I began to discover just how mentally unwell he had been. He had kept so much from me...

I began to wonder if I really knew this man I had been married to for twenty years.

What I did know was as his mental health deteriorated he became increasingly dependent on me for the practical tasks *he* was responsible for. I was getting pulled down with him.

He was sucking the life out of me!

Very few people knew what was going on.

My parents knew I was unhappy yet didn't know the extent of it.

I kept up a good front at work.

I didn't confide in many people (one or two at most) and then didn't fully acknowledge my feelings to myself... let alone anyone else!

Because, hey!

My voice didn't matter!

There had been a couple of occasions when I *had* spoken up in our marriage and been shot down. He was a lost little boy, emotionally, and when, even gently, challenged reacted as an angry toddler and verbally hit out.

I dissolved in tears, which didn't help me in sharing my feelings: standing up for myself.

I was silenced... again!

My voice didn't matter...

I even resorted to writing a letter once so he could read it, and I would be saved from the undermining tears.

He responded with the silent treatment for a week.

My voice didn't matter.

My story, my feelings didn't matter!

Don't get me wrong... there *were* times of joy and laughter in the twenty years we were together.

I also remember him saying to me more than once that I'd be better off without him.

I felt he was rejecting me. He was certainly pushing me away...

Could he see my life zest slowly ebbing away?

As a Christian, I had prayed long and hard for his healing.

I meant my wedding vows: — – in sickness and in health, till death do us part.

His Mam had confronted me with this when he was first signed off work... was I going to leave him??

So now here I am, really starting to feel the tsunami of emotions, of actual physical feelings in my body and the somatic aches and pains that had been dormant for so long...

And yes, relief was in there big time!!

I felt like a prisoner on the day of release from jail!

How could I feel... what was that, happiness? Joy? Relief?

I settled on calling it relief. That was the most socially acceptable.

And yet, I couldn't let on to anyone that was how I felt!

Remember my voice didn't matter!

And then there's the cultural conditioning:

"Don't speak ill of the dead!"

"Don't air your dirty laundry in public!"

"He's not here to defend himself!"

"Don't make a spectacle of yourself!"

"Dignity at all times!"

So now I'm feeling guilt on top of the relief.

I'm feeling guilty that I'm free to live my life for me now!

I'm feeling guilty that in my stubborn loyalty he had to die to release me from our wedding vows!

I'm feeling guilty that I'm relieved the weight suppressing my joie de vivre has been lifted and I can be my quirky, playful, passionate self again!

How could I share this with anyone?

This roller coaster of emotions?

Yes, everyone expects the tears, the "grief" (aka the five recognised stages of denial, anger, bargaining, depression and acceptance).

No one expects joy, happiness even!

Amongst Christian circles, this is more acceptable as we know through faith our loved one is now in heaven…

And yet from the older members of the congregation, I felt the sting of condemnation when a few months later I decided to take off my wedding ring. More cultural mores to navigate…

Though he didn't say it at the time, my brother was taken aback at how "light" I was at the funeral. There's a photo of him and me sitting in the garden after the funeral, and I was not just smiling, I was almost radiant! Mam and Dad loved this photo and had it displayed in their home as they didn't have many photos of the pair of us. When visitors commented my Mam didn't let on the circumstances of that photo, simply that it had been taken in my garden.

She never asked or commented on my lightness that day.

Neither did I!

Some twelve years later, as I was working with my coach, she reflected that I was still working "behind the scenes," working with speakers to get their message out to the world… yet where was I sharing mine? This inner work revealed that long hidden script that "my voice didn't matter." That's when I decided to start sharing my story.

I recorded an in-depth podcast in which the story was told for the first time. Only after hearing that did my brother admit his confusion and that finally, my demeanour on that day made sense!

He couldn't fathom out how I was behaving... he knew he would have been a wreck if his wife of twenty years had died, suddenly or otherwise. Yet he didn't say anything at the time. I wasn't given the opportunity to express my feelings. I didn't offer them, because as you know...

My voice didn't matter!

This podcast was a turning point for me.

In the intervening years (at the time of writing, thirteen years), I have been on such a journey.

I'm reclaiming my innate quirky, playful, passionate self,

I've relocated from Scotland to Australia,

Travelled to new places,

Qualified in Myofascial Release (a form of body work that I use with my speakers too!)

I've started my own business... and what a journey that continues to be!!

I've learnt, and am still learning to be honest, how to feel.

My feelings are important.

When I allow myself to feel them and let them pass through me I acknowledge them and don't deny or suppress them, don't squish them into my body.

I have learnt how to release those pent-up emotions that *have* been stored up in my body... an ongoing process!

I have learnt that my voice DOES matter!

I now speak up and share my story.

In fact, the first time I did so to a group of ladies at a networking meeting one of the audience reached out to me and told me it inspired her to make the decision she had been toying with for some time and to leave her husband as she could so resonate the life being sucked out of her too!

So many of us keep our stories to ourselves...

Except the consequences often leak out in our behaviour.

Geoff was a case in point.

He didn't know how to accept love and pushed me away because he hadn't been loved as a child.

I had my abandonment experience in early childhood, which shaped my life... career in Speech Pathology—which I wouldn't change for a moment!

I also didn't (please note the *past* tense here!) speak up for myself particularly in close personal relationships as I didn't feel my voice mattered.

Discovering that early script, buried deep in my subconscious, has been a turning point in my life. More than fifty years after I first decided my voice didn't matter, it has been a revelation, an awakening, that my voice, my story DOES matter.

I can feel ALL the feels and share the wisdom gained through them with the world.

Will I bare my emotions: real and raw with the world?

Absolutely NOT!

However, for specific people, I'm learning to trust, to open up and share the deeper layers of me.

My voice matters.

My story matters.

So does yours!

And that's why I do what I do now...

Enable people (speakers) to tell *their* stories,

The lessons they have learned,

How they have put into practice the wisdom they have gained through their lived experiences.

You have an audience that wants to be inspired by your wisdom, by your story... you never know the impact your words can have on someone's life.

Maya Angelou famously said, "People will forget what you say, they'll forget what you did but they'll never forget the way you made them feel." Your message, your voice, delivered authentically, in a clear, confident and compelling way will stick with them,

Inspire them

To look at life differently,

Make a change in their behaviour…

It may even save a life!!

I work with people like you, who know you have an important message to share with the world.

You know your experiences have not been simply for you… and you want to save others the same level of pain you experienced.

You have a sense of urgency to leave your legacy mark on the world.

You have a big heart and are being led to help others with your story.

I now have an updated mental script:

"My voice matters!"

My story matters.

So does yours!

If you want to explore how to get your message out to the world, let's talk…

ABOUT WENDY CORNER

Wendy Corner is the founder and creator of Your Words Have Power, a platform for speakers to share their messages and stories to inspire people to live their lives fully. Wendy's on a mission to help countless speakers to step onto stages across the world and share their messages and stories to change lives. Why? Because an unconscious decision made as a two-year-old shaped her life choices. She felt abandoned in hospital and when no one came when she called, she decided that no one else should feel that their voice didn't matter. She developed a passion for communication, even making up her own language as a child. Wendy worked as a Speech Pathologist for almost thirty years in the UK and Australia to enable her clients to have a "voice." Now based in Perth, Australia, she works with international clients who have a burning desire to be speakers from the stage to inspire, motivate, or sell a product/service; who harbour a goal to do a TEDx or wider stage and experience the visibility and credibility being on the red circle brings; who are seeking to launch their career as a prolific professional speaker both in-person and virtually.

FB Groups:
www.facebook.com/groups/courageousinfluentialspeakers
www.facebook.com/corner.net.au/
Email: *wendy@ywhp.events*
Extra Links: *www.linktr.ee/CommCoach*

13

ALLIE XU

A PORTRAIT OF MY LIFE

I have thought long and hard about what I plan to share in this chapter. The most important discovery I have made over the last four years is finding my sense of self. After meeting people from many different walks of life, a universal theme has become apparent to me. A journey to uncover a sense of self and to begin a journey of self-discovery.

OPENING MY DARK BOXES

I was a mess. **Exhausted, defeated, destroyed, bullied, and stepped on are just some of the ways to describe how I felt.** I was lost, silenced, anxious, stressed, and depressed all bundled up into one.

This was me four years ago. Working full-time as a pharmacist at one of the largest hospitals in my state. The irony of the situation was the pride I had working at the time, proud of myself for having a job, the culmination of many years of study. I had a job when positions were hard to come by. It was exciting to be at the center of attention; I felt I was at the hub of activity within the hospital. For some reason, I was filled with a sense of importance, excitement, and anticipation.

Looking back, I would hazard a guess this feeling stemmed from a childhood influenced by my family who had strong medical roots.

My great-grandfather was a well-known Traditional Chinese Medicine doctor. His sons, my grandfather, and my granduncle, were both Western Medicine doctors and both were highly decorated professors in their chosen fields of medicine. My dad and his cousins were all Western Medicine doctors too. Throughout my childhood, there was an expectation I would continue in this vein and carry on the mantle and legacy deeply embedded in my family line.

Even though I was not a medical doctor, working as a pharmacist inside a hospital had given me a sense of belonging. Deep down I struggled with a lack of self-identity and wanted to live up to the expectations and yearned for the approval of my family.

This longing for approval and desire to live up to expectations would have a great influence on me. I still remember how excited I was to begin working in this established and prestigious institution. Little did I realize I had entered a very dark environment with cut-throat individuals, an environment which encouraged unhealthy behaviors. A place of conflict, backstabbing, constant gossiping, and gaslighting creating a toxic and competitive landscape.

The sum of these actions culminated in a workplace plagued by psychological warfare, where privilege and elitism thrived. It was an environment where one was encouraged to look down upon the commoners. Best described in the famous line from the movie The Devil Wears Prada: "millions would kill for that job." In fact, the overall work environment and attitude of the managers and owners are much akin to the behaviors and tendencies of Miranda Priestly.

For a very long time, I was oblivious to the toxic energy resonating from the workplace. I believe it was a combination of ignorance, innocence, and my desire to fit in that blinded me to the unhealthy attitudes held there. As a young pharmacist, new to the industry, there is a certain sense of excitement about entering the workforce. I was ready to give my heart and soul to make a difference.

Little did I suspect that my time would soon be defined by being the workplace punching bag. I received blow after blow, left, right and center. I was left battered and bruised. In a few short years, I had lost my sense of hope, optimism, and the spark in my eyes. I was made to feel smaller and smaller until I was insignificant.

I was at a crossroads; I did not know what to do. I did not recognize the situation I was in. It seemed no matter what I did, the situation only got worse. I tried to engage the power of positive thinking; I tried to be the mediator, the peacemaker, and went out of my way to avoid conflict. Nothing worked. I was lost.

Physically, I was worn out. Mentally, I was exhausted. Spiritually, I was defeated. Emotionally, I was forever traumatized. Yet my lightbulb moment, when I finally came to the realization that I could not change this toxic environment did not occur until I met my husband. He confronted me with the reality that I was trying to fit in at all costs, that I was willing to hand over my autonomy. At that moment I realized I had been stuck in my delusional reality, trying so desperately to live up to my family's expectations to feel excepted. That's when I realized I had to walk away for my life story to truly begin.

A JOURNEY OF SELF DISCOVERY

I still vividly recall my emotions and feelings in the first few days after choosing to leave my job. I had a great sense of relief. Finally, I was safe, liberated from the toxic workplace, and able to breath. At the same time, I was completely drained and exhausted. The adrenaline coursing through my veins, which sustained me in the workplace, had finally dissipated.

Yet that relief was mixed with a sense of uncertainty. My mind started to wander and turned toward thoughts of what was to come next. That sensation of entering the great unknown made my stomach turn as if a host of butterflies had just left their chrysalis. My thoughts turned darker as the cold embrace of self-doubt and fear came rushing in. Everything I had known; my sense of identity came crashing down. The what ifs began piling up in my mind. What if I never find a job again? What if I don't meet my family's expectations? What if I can't make it in the world?

The stream of negative self-talk and voices was unending and overwhelming. I started doubting my choices, wondering if I was weak. Wondering what my family would think of my decisions. Wondering if my in-laws would look down on me. An endless stream of guilt and self-doubt began to take hold.

Clinically, I was diagnosed with chronic fatigue. Emotionally and spiritually, I was depressed and numb. I began to question the meaning of life and of my very existence. I had hit rock bottom.

The good news is when you are at rock bottom, there is only one way to go and that is up. After a period of introspection, reflection and rest I began my quest for solutions. I was inspired by my family. Since my great-grandfather was a Traditional Chinese Medicine doctor, I always had an interest in the art of healing and wanted to fuse this interest with my own culture, values, and traditions. As I gained a greater understanding of Traditional Chinese Medicine, I began my own journey of healing. A journey of self-discovery. I began immersing myself in various healing modalities and in the process uncovered my sense of identity, my one true purpose, and the calling of my soul.

Whilst the process of accumulating knowledge of acupuncture points and adopting Traditional Chinese Medicine theories after leaving a Western Medicine world view was not easy, the most diffi-cult task was reconnecting with my sense of self. The depression, fatigue, and exhaustion drained me of all energy and clouded my hope for a brighter future. Yet I was encouraged by the support of my husband and my family around me. I knew it wouldn't be easy; it was a difficult ordeal. If I wanted to truly embrace the art of healing it was imperative for me to journey through this process and overcome the trauma of my past experiences.

I will not pretend the journey was easy. I was still frustrated, angry, and confused after leaving my previous workplace. I enrolled in numerous courses in the fields of emotional intelligence, psychology, NLP, hypnotherapy, life coaching, nutrition, sound therapy, estab-lishing a successful online business, how to build online courses, human design, coding and more. I signed up for everything I could.

Jumped into meeting after meeting. I was so busy I forgot to eat and sleep. I had become a self-discovery course addict.

I eventually came to the realization that I was filling the void left by leaving my previous workplace. I had become so accustomed to the exhaustion of work and the notion that staying busy is the only way to succeed in life, that I now filled that void with courses that took up all my time. Even though I was now in control of my workday, I was unconsciously filling it to the brim with courses and choosing to push myself to the limit without taking any breaks. The more courses I completed, the more I came to the realization that I was searching for something more. Something within me was still missing. But I was looking externally, what if what I was searching for was internal and within me the whole time?

Through NLP I learned that perception is projection. What we perceive outside ourselves is who we are on the inside. My external world reflected my internal self. My room was cluttered, messy, and busy, which echoed my messy, confused, and cluttered internal world. Through many courses, my mentors would ask me to make changes to my external environment to change my internal world. But no matter how many times I organized and cleaned my room, the mess and clutter would return. The room would return to its natural state of entropy. I realized instead of following the direction of others or a set program, what I needed to find, and follow, was my own innate compass.

With this realization, I decided to turn within myself. I spent less time on electronic devices and social media. I stopped spending time and money on courses and seeking the opinions of others. I started to focus on my innate self and started paying more attention to my thoughts through journaling, meditation, breathing, and getting used to talking about my experiences and feelings. I have realized our thoughts and emotions have profound effects on each other. Thoughts can trigger emotions. And those emotions can then directly affect our physical and mental wellbeing.

HOW OUR BODIES COMMUNICATE

In Traditional Chinese Medicine, these emotions are distilled into five basic categories and linked to a corresponding organ. Anger is aligned with the liver. Fear shares an association with the kidney. Joy is linked to the heart. Sadness and grief are tied to the lung. Whilst worry emanates from the spleen. It is important to pay attention to how we feel and notice our emotions at the same time so we can rebalance ourselves and release negative emotions or energies to avoid any potential damage to our internal organs.

I realized to find a balance we need to find a release mechanism to purge negative emotions. This can be accomplished through shifting our bodies by singing out loud, dancing, screaming in the car, punching a pillow, or joining a boxing class and so on. Since thoughts are innately linked and trigger our emotions, it is imperative to acknowledge and address our thoughts and perspectives. Once I came to this realization, I was able to open a dialogue with my past self by deliberately paying more attention to my day-to-day thoughts and beliefs. Although we cannot recall many events of our childhood, these emotions, and traumatic experiences stay within us. We become a byproduct of these embedded experiences.

My pain was an example of my subconscious mind communicating with my body in the present. Subconscious trauma deeply embedded in childhood was reflected in the conscious pain I was suffering in the present day. In fact, this intimate association between psychological and physical wellbeing is described in many health systems. This integrated health model operates in a dynamic feedback loop where our emotions have a direct impact on our health and vice versa.

As I pay more attention to my body and inner workings, my senses and feelings become more pronounced. After releasing negative emotions, I feel lighter, and my childhood memories also become clearer. I can see things from different perspectives, as my thoughts change, leading to a greater release of emotions. With practice, this has now become second nature. I am enjoying the process. Instead of ignoring my own gut feelings as I would do in the past, I have started to follow and trust my instincts, strengthening my intuition.

I began to respect and take ownership of my feelings instead of reverting to my previous behavior as a people pleaser. I grew more centered and confident in who I am and what I want in life. The lingering doubts and anxiety grew quieter, and in its place, I discovered a newfound confidence and a degree of certainty even when I am out of my comfort zone.

Over time, I allowed myself to feel, express my inner desires, accept who I am, and be who I want to be. Instead of trying to live up to my family expectations. Instead of molding my life to the defining qualities of worldly success. Instead of following the trends and fads of the visible and tangible material world. With this, I have grown more comfortable and confident in my own skin and with who I am.

A PORTRAIT OF MY LIFE

As this chapter draws to a close, I know that I have only just begun to embark upon the journey of a lifetime. Whether as a Traditional Chinese Medicine doctor, a pharmacist, a wife, a daughter, a healer, or the author of my own healing journey I am learning every step of the way. I am grateful for all the kindhearted and like-minded people I have met along the way who have so graciously shared their lessons and experiences with me. I am thankful for the life I lead in this world, and that I have the means to experience and learn the valuable lessons I have shared above. This has been a portrait of my life thus far. If you can identify with experiences I have shared or are in a state of confusion, sadness, frustration, grief, or exhaustion right now, it is my sincere hope that you can start your own journey of self-discovery anew.

Until we meet again.

ABOUT ALLIE XU

Allie is a Traditional Chinese Medicine doctor, pharmacist, and holistic healer. She gains her inspiration from the hero in each of us and fulfils her mission by embracing all optimal modalities for improved vitality and wellness. Her clear understanding of how loving and compassionate energies create space for healing honors her ancestors and future generations. While spending time in the Chinese Medicine Clinic, she also collaborates in the co-creation of culture as a cure, with her involvement in Global Pharmacy Entrepreneurs in addition to acting as the Genius CEO behind Unicorn Fart Media.

In her free time, she enjoys absorbing the rich cultural offerings of her current city of residence, Brisbane, Australia, with her husband and family. She is constantly creating artistic masterpieces, whether in her paintings, singing, or podcast production. Creating safe places for stories to be told and amplifying the importance in each of her relationships.

Websites:
www.alliexu.com
www.unicornfartmedia.com

14

CATHLEENA HAILLEY

The awakened feminine...well, what's that really? I could answer this
question in so many ways, and as I set out to write my chapter for this book,
many versions of what that means to me have shown themselves. What you
are about to read is the final version of all that has come to me. Enjoy!

I **know I chose to come into this world as a female and**
through the parents I ended up with. I know this because
that is who I am and who they are. But what did I choose and why?

As a child I was quite different than most as I was very open,
straightforward, very present, playing, speaking, and showing up just
as I am. The question began, who really am I?

I loved the outdoors, still do, I loved sports, still do and loved to
just play. I never really noticed the differences in others; it was more
of just having fun… until it wasn't, until it became more than that,
until I began to notice more, observing, feeling and hearing things
that were really going on from a very different place than the presence I was used to experiencing.

I was a bit of a tomboy so I played a lot with the boys. I loved a lot
of sports so when they first allowed the girls on a boys' baseball team,
my father decided to have me join in. At first, I loved it, I got to play

first base and I was really good. This lasted about two games until one of the coaches wanted his son in that position so they just pushed me to the outfield. The outfield was the worst position on the team. I didn't realize this at the time but this event would be a foundation of how I experienced myself in the world.

It taught me I was expendable, worthless, unimportant and many other things. During this time in my life, a lot was going on in my world at home—a lot of chaos, too much to share and mostly unimportant to this story. The important part to share was that I had no idea who I really was; I only understood that I knew things and felt things that I didn't know what to do with.

There was a whole other subtle world playing out all around me.

We moved around a bit, and each time seemed harder and more uncomfortable for me to find myself. New awarenesses of who I was kept trying to show up, yet still I was floundering to be self-identified as anything. Honestly, I felt androgynous—just here, but really nowhere.

I was pretty smart so I eventually put myself in college and managed to get a degree in business and a job at the same time. In truth, I started the job when I started college as I had to work to pay for my degree.

I worked for a chiropractor, a woman who was really kind and supportive of me and my journey of self-discovery. Up to this point, I was in my mid-twenties, and I hadn't had anyone really notice me much to take interest in helping me. I wasn't one to ever ask. I felt like life was opening for me during this period until she decided to get married and sell her practice. Everything changed after that. The new chiropractor was quite different, the one good thing that came out of it was that I was guided to go to massage school. You may be wondering how this transition came about? Well, to be honest, I surrendered my misery and decided to go.

You see I continued my college degree while working and was also in a pretty bad relationship with someone who wasn't treating me well at all. To be honest, life really sucked a lot then.

That's really being quite mild about the experience but let's just leave it at that. It was quite the struggle.

Massage came in for me because I was always drawn to the body's mechanics, being athletic and all. My only stumbling block at the time was that I was under the adage "use your brain not your hands" thus the surrendering of my misery became my motivation.

It all turned out to be quite magical; I was introduced to energy. How interesting this became to me. This is where my real story of the awakened feminine begins. You see the truth of where I really am and what is going on started to show itself to me.

I've always been different than most, at least I felt that way. I've spent most of my life in my head, in thought, in observation of the world.

It began very early in life when I noticed all the chaos around me, all the more subtle language spoken from an unspoken perspective.

My family was speaking so loudly yet silently to the physical ears. It was almost maddening hearing and knowing the chaos of others who never really spoke any words.

This was my childhood, my life, sitting within my body, my mind observing a world that was communicating so much to me through what seemed silent. What was happening?

I was a very outgoing person for the first several years of my life, not having much fear of anything, and being adventurous in sports and play. It was my outlet for all the mental chaos around me—if I was outside, my life seemed to expand, it felt free and I could breathe.

I always sought to be outside, and to this day I'm still that way. By being outside, physically just going out of a building, I can expand who I am, I can feel the bigness of myself expanding even bigger and bigger. What does all this mean?

I discovered I was more than this body, much more. There was the *me* within the body, the little human life and there was this other me, the one who is greater than that, the one who was connected to every-thing and felt everything and everyone. Who or what was that me?

My life has been a journey of self-discovery of that me, an awakening of the authentic me. The I AM presence as it is called, my true self. My God or Source self.

I've learned that we are energy, frequency, moving particles of information communicating with each other all the time. This is who I am, this is what has been happening my entire life. The what seemed more subtle communication of energy to all things.

I was aware of what others were really thinking and feeling around me, that they never spoke about, at least in physical words, and somehow I was being puppeted around by what they wanted me to be and do.

I found myself in relationships where I had no real sense of self, no real identity. Always just following someone else, searching for a way to be, not knowing how to be correct or perfect. What was that anyway? It was exhausting. Life was exhausting! Until I finally let go, let go of it all, all the trying to be something, trying to fit in, trying to connect.

Instead, I let go, let go and moved out of my head into my heart. I made a decision to open my heart, to let go of everything, all the dialogue of self, all the self-adjusting all the time for others. What was I doing anyway? I was doing this all inside of me, no one really knew my silent dialogue, my self-monitoring, and my hiding to fit in. Yet somehow I too, my whole life with others, was speaking a very loud silent language and message of who I was and what I wanted. But what was this message I was sending out to the world?

This was a deeper level of awakening, my self-discovery of who I really am, Energy. The real communication of my entire existence. I discovered it was all inside of me, my entire existence was living within this body.

I never really took the time to feel; I spent too much time thinking and observing instead. Opening my heart, meant I was going to feel, feel everything no matter what. This has been my mantra for my life. I am going to keep my heart open no matter what and feel.

Suddenly my real life began, and now I was actually present, in the now moment. I was awake, I became the observer of myself, noticing how I felt around others and what thoughts came into my mind and what sensations came into my body. As I began to observe myself from this now present moment, life began to take on new meaning. I started to feel happy and fulfilled, and I started to feel my purpose for being here.

I discovered who I really am. I am so much more than this physical body. I am energy, Life itself. Life force energy. I am Source.

I became aware that all things are connected through this energy, always communicating with each other. It's what I felt my whole life but couldn't understand. My true life journey has finally begun. I am now ready to get to know who I really am and why I am here. I am finally present to find this out. Awake!

Funny how life shows us our own story if we are willing to notice. When the one who is seeking outward connection to others suddenly realizes, "how would I even know if I was connected, if I have no idea what I am even really feeling," it's like a light suddenly goes on where you didn't even realize there was a light needed in the first place.

I am now awake, to my life, to my journey. As I have become the observer of myself in the physical world, a whole non-physical world has beautifully and magically shown itself to me. I have discovered who I really am, who we all really are, Multidimensional beings. Eternal beings of light and sound.

As I allowed the subtle to become known, my life suddenly began to make sense. There were things I always knew but couldn't explain how or why I knew them. Now I could see, feel, and know the truth.

My life now is so far from where I began but ironically it has come full circle.

You see I realized that the discovery of myself as energy was not really new at all. In fact, it was what I knew and how I lived my entire life. It was why I lived in a world inside myself. My discovery of letting go and moving into my heart brought me into the physical reality. So now my true adventure finally wearing this human suit has begun.

I never knew how to be human; how to be a person in the world; who I was. Now through my awakening, I am on a quest to be the most authentic, Multidimensional being I can be. It's really quite beautiful.

I guess what I really want to say is that through what seemed an outward message I learned the truth of who I have been, who I truly am and why I am here at this time.

I am here to awaken to who I truly am so that I may become an example of the reality of who we really are and what amazing possibilities truly exist. Life is a beautiful adventure of being who you are and discovering your own uniqueness through authentic present-moment experiences.

That's it!

So what exactly was this I AM presence and who had I discovered I truly am?

Well, when reflecting on my childhood, I had remembered that as my parents spoke something, when I was really little, I could hear what came from their mouths with my physical ears, but at the same time I heard something else in my head and then I felt even something different from both things I heard. It was all quite confusing. This is why I believe I retreated to my mind. It seemed less complicated.

As I developed and this sort of thing became my normal, I later realized that I was listening to the conversations people were speaking and asking from their heads. This is why I became a chameleon and felt puppeted around. It made it really hard to not only be myself but to be around anyone I felt I could even be myself at all, as I had begun to realize who really was myself anyway?

As I practiced observing myself around others, I noticed that something would happen when I approached people. As I let myself start to be present, my energy would send out a message that as I observed was allowing or causing the truth of who that person was in the depths of their own energy to come to the surface.

Some people liked this and some did not. The ones who did began to tell me their life stories in great detail and personal depth. I found this interesting as this happened often in casual encounters or first encounters with people. Those who didn't like this would shut down, pull away and show a definite dislike for me.

The whole thing was quite uncomfortable as I found people were expressing either need for me or disdain for me. Either way, I couldn't seem to find the neutral ground in most relationships.

The ones who expressed need led me to discover what was really happening.

I discovered what is now referred to as the Zero point. This, in energy, is the present moment without judgment or the place of nothing and all possibilities. I noticed that I was showing up as this zero point and in fact, that is where my energy lives so to speak. Once I recognized this about my energy, I started to also be aware that I, Cathleena, needed to be in the zero point or heart space, as this is where we in the human body experience this all the time, or I would keep having the experiences of people either needing me or showing disdain for me.

As I practiced being in the zero point or heart space, I started to get to know who I was as this multidimensional being. I recognized all the unspoken language I had experienced my whole life starting to speak very clearly and profoundly to me. I became aware I was understanding—or as I like to say: *inner standing*—the nature of myself as energy and frequency. In fact, I was quite knowledgeable.

I learned I have had many existences, some not on this planet and that I came here specifically in this lifetime to embody my full source self to represent the original human blueprint. Which is way more than anything we have been taught about human anatomy and physiology.

I now have a regular practice in which I assist others in private and group sessions to awaken to who they really are as multidimensional beings. I refer to myself as a frequency alchemist as I am able to see, feel, hear, and be aware of all facets of a human's existence through what is referred to as the quantum field. My contribution to their awakening is to release frequencies and energies that they have aligned to that are not authentic to who they are so that they can show up as who they really are.

You see we are already unique aspects of source consciousness. All we have to do is be ourselves. It's that easy and that complicated at the same time. Only because we have been living in a world that tries to deny that energy and frequency exist and that there is a hidden communication going on all the time, only hidden by the living in the mind instead of the heart.

As we all move from our minds into our hearts, a whole other beautiful existence shows itself and life becomes magical.

We are amazing beings of light, sound and love. We are creator beings. That is, we create our own existence through our experience. Enjoy the process of getting to know yourself, the amazing you as I am.

As you move from your head to your heart, you will notice how life becomes magical! It is with the most incredible expansion of my heart that I speak these words to you with gratitude for this opportunity to share this small bit of my story.

I have so much excitement and anticipation for what kind of world will show up from all you amazing creator beings.

From my heart to yours I am sending so much love. Until we speak again…..

ABOUT CATHLEENA HAILLEY

Cathleena Hailley is an embodiment of the divine feminine who works with the Council of 9 Collective and in particular with Jesus, Metatron, and other ascended masters. As the lineage of the life Architect, her Crystalline DNA signature not only carries the frequency of perfect pitch to align to the original Human templet, Earth templet and this Universes templet but continually recalibrates this alignment. Having incarnated as an Arcturian, Andromedan, and as a member of the Council of 9 Galactic Collective, Cathleena brings the knowledge of human patterns of existence, along with her extensive knowledge and work with interplanetary and galactic portals. Through this, she accesses human patterning with galactic information, technologies and energies to fully access their original soul's blueprint. Cathleena has a business degree and has worked with many professionals and medical practitioners in her massage therapy practice for over twenty-eight years; she has experienced layers of human patterning, personalities, and life expressions. Her background in massage, using techniques such as Rolfing and Myofascial, has allowed her to begin to access more subtle energies connected to the emotional patterning that creates an individual's life.

Website: www.cathleenahailley.com
Email: cathleenahailley@gmail.com
Facebook: www.facebook.com/cathleenahailley

15

CELESTE PALMER

I have many stories that have led me to this very moment I sit in as I write this. Although the experiences were often hard to endure and accept, I am grateful for them all for they have helped shape and expand me into the Woman I am today.

$\mathcal{M}$y journey towards awakening began after a divorce in 2017. However, now in hindsight and more fully Integrated within myself, it's clear to me that my story begins long before he decided I wasn't the woman he wanted anymore. So I'll start there—from the beginning...

I grew up running amongst the tall Evergreen trees of the Great Pacific NorthWest. Some of my most vivid memories are of my younger self, running wild through the woods, in blind trust as my chin-length hair covered my face and eyes although never slowing me down. I was the youngest of four kids in a home filled with an abundance of love and loss. I stopped asking the question "why" a long time ago when I realized that the three-letter word took me nowhere but deeper into the suffering of a question with no answers.

When I was nine years old, my twin sister Caitlin was diagnosed with leukemia, a cancer of the blood. By the age of twelve, we hardly looked like sisters anymore. Her hair had fallen out, her face and body swollen with extreme inflammation, and her eyes and skin yellow from organ failure. When we were thirteen, she slipped into a coma before passing away under the white fluorescent lights of the children's hospital in Seattle. It's hard to say if the cancer killed her or rather the four long years of harsh western medicines.

I lost the rest of my family in a way that day too. The death of a daughter, little sister and twin sister pushed us all to fall apart, shut down, turn off or run away in our own ways. That was the day I fell asleep for a very long time, under the weighted blanket of sadness from her absence.

My father became physically and mentally ill within a few years of my sister's passing. His grief and rage of having to attend his own daughter's funeral before his own eventually manifested as cancer in his body too, and madness in his mind. During his final weeks of life, I sat next to his hospice bed in my grandmother's living room, with stacks of books on food as medicine. Although I could hardly get through the first chapters, I was barely alive myself. My heart and spirit were sick then too.

All those years ago, before knowing what I know today, I had an innate sense of awareness that we could heal ourselves. That my father's healing was possible. But what to do and how to move forward, I was stuck.

After almost two full decades of sleeping through my waking life, it was the third strong shock to my heart that sparked my awakening. My relationship of seven years, a marriage where I had compromised my own dreams for his, had ended. I was alone but what was worse was that I had lost myself in the other. I had lost my own World in his World. But perhaps I was already lost and absent in Self when he found me.

I remember laying in a dark sad room, surrounded by the untouched boxes of my old life. I had barely moved in days. Broken on the floor of my strange new bedroom. Lost and uncertain of how to pick myself up to begin again. The weather matched my mood. It had been raining for days but I hadn't noticed—I was too consumed by the dull ache of my heavy heart and the pounding confusion in my head.

A loud stern voice that wasn't my own, spoke! "It's time to get up. Go outside" it said. Then as if I was picked up off the floor, I grabbed my coat and shoes before stepping outside for the first time in days. When I opened the front door, a perfectly full rainbow arched directly out in front of me. I began to weep again this time with hope. It was a tangible moment of magic. A blessing that colored my gray sky with Spirit. God had given me a clear message, and all of me knew that everything was okay. That I was being held and that this too would pass. I had been revived, living again with trust in my heart.

The rest of my life continued to move forward the way it always does. Monday through Friday I sat behind a desk at my nine-to-five corporate sales job with a feeling that had, unfortunately, become too familiar. I was deeply unfulfilled and dreading going to work most mornings. It felt like holding my breath until Friday came, then my weekends were gone before I could fill my lungs back up again.

I knew deep within my being that there was more for me than the experience I found myself living in and a feeling of urgency grew strong inside of me. The discomfort of the dissonance between my innate essence and my current expression of life eventually grew so strong that I felt the only thing I could do was change. To let go of all the old remaining pieces of my life that I was still holding onto. I remember the day I made the decision to quit my job. It felt as if my energy was stifled right out of me the moment I sat behind my desk, surrounded by the cubicle's short white walls. Although I wasn't sure of my next steps, after I committed to this a series of divinely orchestrated doors began to open for me. My pipeline filled with a few large deals affording me the possibility to fulfill an almost lost childhood dream of spontaneous travel and wandering the World. This would nurture my Sagittarius rising and my sleeping Spirit would awaken again.

So I followed the pull of my broken but wild heart and with a tummy full of butterflies I took a big leap of faith, and with my arms wide open I fell into the great unknown. I broke my lease, sold my car along with most of my belongings and bought a one-way ticket to Mexico where I would land my curious feet on the astrocartography line of my Natal Moon, to nurture my inner child.

A week before leaving my city at the time, after my final yoga class in Austin, Texas, I met a gentleman who would randomly begin telling me about his life-changing experience in the Amazonian Jungle. Although in Truth, I know there was nothing random about that meeting. I remember clearly to this day, the moment the word slithered off his tongue. All of me heard it, including my sleeping Spirit. I felt it rattle my bones as it landed front and center of my consciousness, and I believe this Mysterious Medicine began working with me the very moment I heard her name.

Ayahuasca....

About three months into my travels, now in Europe, I had arrived at a retreat where I would sit in my first series of ceremonies that would catapult me deep into my forgotten wounds for healing and awakening and light for me a new path. I had been asking myself for years leading up to this experience the burning question that all seekers eventually ask themselves: "What is my purpose?" not knowing it would finally be answered here. During my third ceremony, my path and my purpose had been revealed to me and in deep gratitude, I bowed in the dark as I had found my Medicine, my Teacher, my Therapy, and my Church.

During one of my very first ceremonies, while floating in the ethers outside of time and space, the Shaman leading those ceremonies who would later become my human teacher of this lineage, sang Sacred Medicine Songs that carried me on a profound journey into my future. I watched myself walk barefoot into the Jungle beneath a big Moon sky full of stars glittering against the darkness of the night. A single flower grew out from each of the footprints I left behind me as I stamped myself into the wet Earth that I walked upon. I felt this was an invitation to the lands where Ayahuasca grows native. An invitation to the Amazon. When I understood this, the Medicine rapidly took me even further out into my future. I was shown my old wise Self with long gray hair tied into a bun on top of my head, singing Sacred songs of the Earth through aged wrinkled lips, while I rattled a bundle of leaves in my right hand. I saw myself now as the Shaman leading ceremony.

That night, the benevolent spirit of Ayahuasca showed me my potential. That vision spun me up and out of this World where I danced amongst the stars before I lost my footing. When I returned from that expansive trip, I was overwhelmed with both excitement and responsibility. There was so much space between where I was and what I had been shown. The journey ahead felt long and daunting, but I couldn't unsee what I had seen that night in ceremony. There was no going back. In fact not moving forward would only increase the already present discomfort and dis-ease of living a life that was out of alignment with my Divine Truth. And so it would begin, the process of aligning myself with that big, beautiful vision.

So as she does, Ayahuasca unlocked and opened the doors to the darkest caverns hidden within my psyche. The places I needed to visit within myself before I could rise up to that big beautiful vision. She illuminated everything that was preventing me from embodying my Higher Purpose as Curandera and Shaman of Light. I became highly triggered and reactional. My core wounds, the ones that were most unconscious to me, were now coming forward to finally be seen, heard, felt and loved. Ironically I found myself in the perfect environment for those wounds to be triggered in all the ways necessary to finally make them conscious again. Like a child having a tantrum, I was. Dragging my dreadful shadow around and projecting it onto others as if it was anything but my own. That's what a wounded little girl looks like. Ayahuasca had literally popped the lid off my wounds as deep as the Ocean. She brought my hell right up and out of me so that I was living in it in real time. I had been activated. I was shook up. I was awakened.

You see, healing is a process and often things may seemingly get worse first before they begin to get better. This is the healing crisis or the "die-off" that happens when getting well, which is exactly what began next for me on my journey of healing and awakening. The disintegration before the integration and falling apart before coming together again in wholeness. My path of healing had truly only just begun. I had barely entered into the incubation period of chrysalis. I was at the beginning of the space between the old and the new. The complete dissolving of old cellular structures to transform myself into a new, unrecognizable expression of Self. A complete and total metamorphosis. A remembering of my Essence.

Ayahuasca had shocked my heart alive again and I could no longer sleep through the gift of life I was given.

Six months later, after receiving the invitation into La Selva (the jungle), I arrived in a small town above the Amazonian River of Peru where I would enter into my first of many Shamanic Master Plant Diets to begin learning in the traditional way, directly from the Plants themselves.

"La Dieta" is a Sacred practice where an individual goes into complete solitude for some time, following strict disciplines in exchange for healing and learning. Some of these disciplines include eating a very simple, plain and neutral diet, living in solitude by oneself, not communicating or making contact of any kind with others, no physical touch or sexual exchange with self or others, no consumption of information through media, writings, text etc. These offerings create a pure, uninterrupted channel to connect with and bridge a relationship between the person and the plant. This is a process of both emptying ourselves and filling ourselves up again with the healing frequency of the Master Plant Medicines of the Amazon; Sophia Gaia's Sacred pharmacy.

These plants would crack me so far open so the same light that conceived of me could penetrate me and clean all the parts of myself that had been swallowed by the weighted shadow of my grief.

I would come to grow in love with these Medicines and fall into deep trust and unwavering belief in them. They became my teachers, doctors, guides and allies. These plants have made me stronger physically, mentally, emotionally and spiritually. They have expanded my heart and consciousness and have prepared me to carry these Sacred Earth Medicines responsibly and with immaculate integrity, through my unique blueprint for the deep cellular purification within humanity and Sophia Gaia. For the deep cellular purification within ourselves and our Divine Mother Earth.

About half a year later, after completing my first Master Plant Diet, an introduction into this World of Mystery and Medicine, I returned again to La Selva to continue deepening my studies with these Sacred Plant Intelligences of the Amazon. After spending two weeks dieting with a Master plant named Chiric Sanango, during my closing ceremony Ayahuasca led me on a journey towards making a decision for myself. My teacher's simple clothing began to transform until he was covered from head to toe with an intricate headdress of feathers, slowly walking through the space now as a large human bird. The rattling of his chakapa, a shamanic instrument made out of a big bundle of leaves, orchestrated the feathers to begin folding into themselves before they folded me too, pulling me into a downward spiral. I slid fast through the trunk of an elephant that shot me into another World glowing with vibrant colors unlike anything I'd ever seen before. I pressed my hands up against a window that prevented me from stepping through, and I saw into a dimension where the secrets of the Universe live encoded in the hidden world of Earth consciousness. Like an innocent child, I gasped in awe telepathically communicating with the Spirit of Ayahuasca. "WOW! Is this your World?!?" I asked? Then before I could go any further into it, and just as fast as she brought me down there, she sucked me back up and out again, and like a labyrinth led me on a journey through my own Psyche so I could work to harmonize the conflicting thoughts of uncertainty around a very specific and big decision. A decision that would forever change my life and initiate me into an extraordinary vision, a significant purpose, and an ancient lineage. Ayahuasca didn't do anything TO me or tell me to do anything at all. Rather she guided me to find the answers within myself. Then after dissolving fear and working around perceived limitations and blocks, I arrived with all of me in total cohesion. My heart spoke and I declared to Her, Myself and God "I would be honored to sing in ceremony!" After that declaration, the effects of the Medicine vanished instantly and the ceremony finished shortly after.

When I returned to my private casita, I entered into another experience for deep, quantum healing. Through my own healing, I watched the spirit of my deceased father heal. It was like he was there with me in my little casita, going through his own process of healing through La Dieta. I observed him express and move through massive rage, then deep sadness and grief before finally reaching acceptance and peace.

It was this night I deeply understood that when we heal ourselves, we are healing beyond time. I witnessed how through my own desire, will and effort to heal myself I was assisting in the healing of my family line too. Both forward and back and throughout all places and spaces between and beyond. That experience proved to me that what we do truly matters and when we heal ourselves we absolutely contribute to the healing of others and the healing of the collective whole.

The most important initiation is the Self-initiation through saying YES to our Self.

That following morning, after a sleepless yet profound night, I had one of the most magical and unforgettable moments of my life when I received a beloved and cherished gift from La Selva. Because I had said yes to a vision, I received my first Icaro, a Sacred Medicine song and hymn that the Jungle sang for me so that I could sing it for others in my own future ceremonies.

Healing is hard; however, not healing is even harder. Perhaps the most valuable lesson and tool I have acquired throughout my journey of awakening has been the simple Medicine of Gratitude. And as I continue to peel back the many layers of density I carry until the point I choose to let them go, it's finding whatever sliver of gratitude I can that allows me to surrender and open. And it's only when we surrender to a deeper degree can the Light enter us to help us heal through our pain and suffering.

So if you take anything away from my story of awakening, I hope it's Gratitude. Gratitude even when it hurts. In fact, Gratitude especially when it hurts.

ABOUT CELESTE PALMER

Celeste Palmer is an Intuitive Transformational Guide, Sacred Sound and Cellular Alchemist, and Curandera of traditional medicine of the Amazon.

Shaman of Light, Celeste is here to assist in the resurrection of the Divine Feminine Sophianic template within humanity and Sophia Gaia.

Through her channeled wisdom and sacred sound codes, she assists others in melting away many layers of cellular imprints of separation, fear, and distortion within the physical, mental, emotional, and spirit bodies.

Celeste works with the Unconscious Mind to guide others towards increased Self-awareness so they can heal from traumas, release stuck emotions, expand beyond disempowered belief systems and consciously create their desired reality.

Weaving a combination of both ancient and modern tools and technologies, Celeste has long been on a quest, seeking ways to be in service to All.

Guided by spirit and grounded in neuro-psychology, she empowers individuals to greater embody their Divine Truth, Sacred Sovereignty, and Higher Purpose.

Website: www.celestepalmercoaching.com
Instagram: www.instagram.com/celestepalmer

16

ISABEL REGINA ESMANN

ACKNOWLEDGEMENT

My chapter in the co-creation of The Awakened Feminine: Stories of Women Awakening to Who They Truly Are is dedicated to my husband Jochen and our children Finia and Luis. Thank you for creating, sharing, and committing to this lifetime with me. Through you and with you I can truly experience my divine feminine as a woman, wife and mother. Thank you; I love you so much.

INTRODUCTION

My intention in sharing my story is to inspire women to step into —and fully live—their divine feminine, honor and welcome the divine masculine, and together create the life of their dreams. My story also introduces Chinese philosophies such as Taiji Quan and Fengshui as tools to balance yin (feminine energy) and yang (masculine energy).

The chapter is divided into different parts, showing my awakening and embodying the divine feminine throughout different stages in my life and continuing to do so to form a bigger picture in every step I take.

HONORING THE DIVINE MASCULINE

Around my thirties, I was living what I would describe at that time as a successful life. My career as a real estate leasing manager was going great. I closed deals one after another and one better than the other. I was financially independent and abundant.

But whenever I closed the door to my apartment in the evening after a long day at the office, I could no longer hold back the tears. No longer could I brush aside the emptiness and loneliness inside. No one to share all the great successes, the hours, and life outside of the office walls.

I was financially successful but emotionally unfulfilled.

When a dear friend and colleague invited me for a few weekends of coaching, I turned her down, believing that she needed coaching, not me.

Until one evening.

I was driving back home from the office when I misinterpreted a red light as a green light and crashed my car into a row of cars that had stopped at the traffic lights.

I stepped out of the car. I was fine, and thankfully, no one was hurt.

As I looked at my damaged car, I told myself that not only was the car a full wreck, but my entire life was a full wreck too!

I needed no more. I signed up for a coaching program under Maria and Stephan Craemer, the founders of Contextuelles Coaching®, which my friend had suggested and I had refused for a long time.

I was successful but without fulfilment. No lasting or serious relationships with men. No one to share all the great successes I achieved on a business level.

I loved financial success and also being with and around men but at a safe distance.

To my astonishment, the coaching program went beyond the usual tips and tricks on how to improve your life. Throughout the program, we all had the chance to hold a dialogue with the coaches and figure out what was the deep, deep belief that held us back from reaching our desired goals and manifesting the life of our dreams.

Mine was that virility is dangerous. Until then, it was not obvious to me because I was financially successful but couldn't live in a relationship with a man and financially I had to admit that I had months before my bank account balance was a negative figure. The realization and acknowledgement were the first steps but were not enough. The shifting to a new possibility—virility is fulfilling—and the true embodiment of this new possibility the next.

Each participant of the coaching program presented the old inner belief and the new possibility to the other attendees. Having statements for both sides and presenting that each side was the ultimate truth. Of course, neither of the sides was the ultimate truth but a possibility to live in, being the base from which we create results.

The process of fully embodying the new possibility by living and being this statement was so freeing and transformational beyond words. It opened an entirely new space and level to my life.

A test came on our way back home, which of course was not part of the coaching program but how the universe unfolded to us—a possibility for us to further expand or not.

I had been sharing my car with four other attendees for the past few weekends. I had insisted on driving the entire 600 km to and from the location of the program.

About 30 minutes into our journey home, I exited the highway to the gas station to fill the car with gas. As I walked back to the car after paying, I heard a clear and determined voice inside, saying, "Hand over the keys. Hand over the keys."

I paused for a second and then asked the only man driving with us if he would be willing to drive the car home. He and the other three looked at me in astonishment since this had never happened before. He of course agreed.

I got in next to the driver, and we continued our way home. We were all happily chatting and sharing our experiences from the weekend then out of nothing, a huge deer jumped from the middle side rail of the three-lane highway, crashing into the front side of the car and onto the hood, smashing the front window. Bam!

We were all shocked because we couldn't explain how a deer could come from the middle side rail of the highway. It was as if it just came out of nothing, just for us. Thankfully, our driver had held on to the driver's wheel, continuing straight ahead. I knew instantly if I had been the driver I would have steered the car to one or the other side. Oh, imagine what could have happened.

No one was hurt. We were all safe.

All of us in the car had a major realization in our lives.

Our driver who had been diagnosed with MS said he was strong enough to handle a car crash and keep everyone safe; a single mom who hadn't called her ex-husband for help in years called and asked if he would pick up their daughter from kindergarten because she wouldn't make it on time; the other two women and I realized that we were safe with men and could trust in men, and we expanded our commitment to live in a happy and fulfilling relationship.

COMMITTING TO THE NEW POSSIBILITY

I realized that everything in life is a reflection of our inner beliefs. A co-creation.

Even your home is a reflection of your inner beliefs.

Take a look at where and how you are living—which results you have achieved and which ones you haven't. Look at your habits and reactions.

With all I knew and found out about myself throughout the coaching program and setting my goal for living a happy and fulfilling relationship, I invited a Fengshui consultant to have a look at my home to adjust my living environment to the results I wanted to gain in life.

A happy, fulfilling relationship, children and family.

She stepped into my apartment and said, "Oh, my god. In which fear are you looking?"

I had placed two big black leather sofas into the room according to Fengshui representing relationship and marriage. The sofas were taking over the majority of the space.

My bedroom was in the space standing for fortune and for the most effective direction financially.

The area representing the younger generation and children wasn't even present in the floor plan of the apartment because it belonged to the neighboring apartment.

That is what my life represented—financially abundant but without a fulfilling relationship, marriage, or children in my life.

She asked me to change my bedroom and living room, to remove the black sofas.

It was not about adjusting or changing furniture: it was about your inner beliefs. Fengshui in addition made it obvious through my living environment.

The realization of what your inner beliefs are, the shifting of your inner beliefs, and embodying the new possibility is the true change. Using all the tools I learned through attending the coaching program, I was ready to see and have the results in my life. I sold my sofas and changed my bedroom to the living room. Refurnished, redecorated.

I had enough and sought the results in my life that I desired and wanted to manifest.

I made the decision that it was enough, that I would meet my future husband and live in a fulfilling relationship.

A dear friend of mine invited me to a home gathering and casual party. On the day of the event, I woke up with a severe migraine. My head hurt on the left side, the side referred to as the feminine side. I knew I had to go. The inner calling and voice was bigger than all the excuses my mind came up with and bigger than the resistance that shone through my physical pain. My intention was greater than the limitations and barriers.

Yes, there he was, chatting with the husband of my friend who invited me to the party. Chatting about wincers producing prosecco and champagne. I turned my head as my future husband talked about his favorite champagne.

I knew instantly that was him. The one I selected to play big with and create and enjoy my life with. Manifesting family, children and success, being financially successful and emotionally fulfilled—which I hadn't been until then.

It wasn't all smooth straight away. We had to overcome some commitments but stayed committed and that was the most important.

HONORING THE DIVINE FEMININE

We married, became parents of two wonderful children and embarked on a great adventure together, moving to China as our daughter was eight weeks old.

The beginning of my true inner calling and essence. Surrendering to my feminine essence and stepping more and more into natural laws taught in martial arts and Fengshui. The continuing path to my awakening that had already ignited.

I didn't work in China; I stayed home caring for and looking after my family and organizing our family life. I had just become a mom. I stayed home. I didn't speak the language or read the language.

A time of surrendering. Being open, present, and receptive. First of all, becoming pregnant and then devoting myself and surrendering to motherhood. Stepping out of being a businesswoman focused on results to enjoying the process. Reversing result oriented-ness to process-oriented daily procedures. Understanding the needs of my baby girl without words and understanding the people around me without speaking the language. Becoming more and more reliable on my intuition and surrendering to being guided by that inner voice. Being aware, compassionate, nourishing, caring, and bonding. Welcoming more and more the feminine energy I had suppressed for a long time, trying to compete in the business world—commercial real estate—run mostly by men. Trying to be the better man as a woman.

Was it easy? No.

It took me quite some effort to stop functioning in the masculine energy, which is natural to men; not women. We can access the masculine energy in us, but it takes us, women, a lot of energy.

So, it was such a blessing for me that I wasn't allowed to work in China. It enabled me to fully be a wife to my husband and mother to my children. To fully focus on them and enjoy my life by trying out new activities that interested me.

ONENESS

In the first quarter after arriving in China, I joined a calligraphy workshop, interested in diving into and learning Chinese culture. The master wrote two Chinese calligraphy banners and said, "After the course, I will hand one of each to one of you."

The master chose me to receive one of the two banners. Mine said, "Jing Qi Shen" – the three treasures

At that time I didn't know that this was a sign of my future path unfolding for me. An important basis of Traditional Chinese Medicine, Daoism, Taiji Quan, Fengshui. Tapping into synchronicity unfolding further in my life.

In Chinese, the word crisis also stands for chance. And so for me, it was a chance as the world changed and countries went into lockdown in 2020.

My children's kindergarten closed for the first half of the entire year.

As soon as parks reopened, I took the children out into the park with a friend of mine early in the morning after our husbands left for work.

In China, the parks are full of activities—people running, exercising, dancing, playing cards, connecting to nature, tapping; activating the flow of energy in your body through hitting onto pressure lines, releasing blockages and of course, practicing Taiji Quan.

I paused daily at the main Taiji square and watched for a while, fascinated by the harmonious movements of the Taiji Quan practitioners and calming and grounding atmosphere.

One morning one of the eldest stepped out of the practice and said in Chinese, that they do Taiji, and asked if I wanted to join.

Yes! I had no question about it at all. I wanted to join. I wanted to take the opportunity.

My friend said, "Go. I'll take the children to explore the park. Go 😊."

Excited, I accepted and joined.

I followed the movements of my master Yan Jing Rui standing in front of the group as well as the movements of the group, returning weekly and later on a daily basis. At first, it was only copying and mimicking the movements of the master.

Throughout my daily practice I got an awareness of the theory and state of mind. The more I practiced the calmer and harmonized I got. My body was getting stronger, replenishing my Qi through a healthy and strong body and elevating my consciousness.

- JING QI SHEN -

Now looking back, I can say I am fascinated by how one's path unfolds. As the calligraphy master gave me the banner, I didn't know what it meant. Through my practice, I understood the essence of it: a sign revealing my purpose, directing my path.

I was accepted by Master Yan Jing Rui as his student, cultivating more and more the ancient theory of Taiji Quan. He taught me the different styles of Taiji Quan Martial Arts—Yang, Wu, Chen, Taiji Sword and Taiji Fan.

From an outsider's view, Taiji Quan can be interpreted as pure masculine energy, interpreting that its existence solely comes from a fighting situation.

Taiji Quan is an art of inner cultivation, harmonizing yin and yang, feminine and masculine energy internally. There is no yang without yin and no yin without yang. Yin and yang already being the separation of oneness.

The Daoist honors feminine energy. Referring to a mythical story, the Goddess Guan Yin, a Daoist deity, showed up before Xuan Wu as he was bathing in the river to clear his organs from sins and emotional ballast. Xuan Wu was blessed with immortality for his devotion and his organs were transformed into the symbol of a snake and turtle. God Xuan Wu is referenced as a deity of Martial Arts.

The origin of Taiji Quan is not fully distinguishable.

The Daoist closely watched nature and its inhabitants to incorporate universal laws into their being and living habits. The different styles evolved from and through different masters throughout the years and generations.

One morning practicing I was able to come back to oneness. It is impossible to describe oneness since the attempt to define oneness is still separation.

My lower body grounded and connected to the earth, focusing on my lower dantian, the upper body light and the mind still. No chatter in my head, no drifting away of thoughts, solely in the now and connected to the sky. The movements came easily, no more thinking, no more form, no more style. Solely one with all. A state of flow and ease. A breakthrough in my practice, in my inner cultivation of this ancient art.

I used the opportunity of living in China to find out more about Fengshui.

I was introduced to Master Liao Jianbing, a doctor of Traditional Chinese Medicine who already owned his own clinic at the age of thirty. His grandfather shared with him ancient wisdom from a young age.

Master Liao Jianbing accepted me as his student as he noticed that I understood the meaning and essentials of his teachings without sharing the same spoken language.

If you want to win outside, you first have to cultivate peace inside. Master Liao Jianbing interpreted Yi Jing, the ancient book of changes. And so it was.

As inside as outside. Both are directly linked, interconnected. No one without the other.

MY CALLING

So here I am now back in Germany and feeling called to share my story, as well as the wisdom of ancient traditions, gained living abroad. Taiji Quan and Fengshui.

I'm sharing my story so that the ones resonating with any of the content mentioned can connect and use this for their benefit to achieve their goals and live the fulfilling life they desire.

Being a stand for embodying the true essence of our being and the fusion of masculine and feminine energies to find oneness within us all.

We are nature and energy and there is no separation.

I dearly thank my coaches and masters, all who contributed and empowered me to find the answer: all is one. It is an honor to learn from you and that you share your wisdom with a broader society.

"WHEN YOU DO THINGS FROM YOUR SOUL, YOU FEEL A RIVER MOVING IN YOU." - Rumi

ABOUT ISABEL REGINA ESMANN

Isabel Regina Esmann is married and the mother of a daughter and son.

She moved to China with her husband and eight-week-old daughter in 2016, and their son was born in Shenyang China in 2019.

She devoted her free time to learning and studying ancient wisdom such as Taiji Quan and Fengshui while living abroad.

Isabel empowers women and men to step into their natural divine feminine and masculine energy using the above-mentioned philosophies.

Empowering to create conscious living and working spaces to evolve to the next level defined through her engagement as a real estate agent.

Website: *www.esmannrealeste.com*
Email: *i.esmann@esmannrealestate.com*
Facebook: *www.facebook.com/isabel.esmann.77*

KATHLEEN QUIGLEY

BECOMING THE LIGHT I AM

As I begin to write about my journey of expansion into the I Am, I pray for clarity, love and divine wisdom to guide me. The Divine Feminine immediately pops in and says, "You got this! We are here now showing up in multitudes to support one another on this journey of divine love and empowerment. Go for it!!!" So here I go.....

Heart of the Wild Flower:

> *I Am the Energy of the Wild Flower*
> *I grow Wild*
> *I grow Free*
> *I sow Seeds of Freedom on this Earth*
> *Follow My lead to your True Nature*
> *Wild and Free*
> *Manifest it Now*
> *Be Free!*

*M*y journey has been one of expansion, step by step. In this lifetime, it has been divided up into three timelines. That of my birth until the age of twenty-seven, age twenty-seven to age fifty, and age fifty-one to the present time. The rebirth that has taken place each time is a new beginning of my expanded, true self. Each phase holds significant beauty and wisdom, which once embodied brings me to the next. Each cycle blends into the next, melding that which has fragmented off back into the Divine Oneness of the Unity that I Am. I am grateful for it all…the sadness, the joy, the intense grief and the immense bliss. Each holds its sacred medicines and stories that weave a multi-colored tapestry that is uniquely Me. I'm guided to share three of my stories of divine empowerment with you now. May this nourish and empower the seeds of your Divine Soul Print!

I am an artist, first and foremost. What I mean by that is art is and has always been my first language, and I find words and speaking to be much more difficult. The creative process centers me and holds me in my open heart space and is an energetic channel guiding me through its unspoken mysteries. Throughout this life journey, art has been my dearest companion. In my younger years, my love of the creative process saved my life and as I have grown the creative process has opened me up in vastly different ways. The creative process is magical alchemy. It is the trinity of you, the creative process and the divine spirit that interacts and manifests the magic that is an expression and expansion of Creator You! We have been programmed to believe that the creative process is not of any importance in our everyday existence. Creativity is so much bigger than a process relating to the arts. Creativity is the language of the heart. Creativity is our birthright. We are born in an act of creation and we are born in the image of our divinely unique creator self. We are the master creator and our life is our masterpiece. I am and always will be a champion of the creative process, as it brings forth the beautiful cycles/gateways of birth, death, and rebirth.

The first story I will share is one of dying and rebirth…on many levels and in many ways.

I was thirty-eight years old, married for the second time with a seven-year-old son and three older step-children. I had married what I believed was my soul mate five years prior. He was also my teacher in an esoteric school of The Fourth Way. I had started and was implementing an Art Therapy program at Children's Hospital, had my art career exhibiting and selling art, teaching alongside my husband, and basically running as fast as I could to avoid my higher self and my divine wisdom. Although I was a "student" of higher consciousness, I now see my center of gravity was in people-pleasing and fear of my true nature, who I truly was. I could feel myself when I was painting, that was the crack that always let the light in but I made sure my life was so jam-packed that I was only with myself and in my studio one day a week. I would not allow myself to be alone with the Alone of me. I was in hiding most of the time and giving my power away constantly.

It was right before Thanksgiving and I had a mammogram appointment. I decided I was too busy and rescheduled for after the holidays into the new year. As I sat in the waiting room I had a knowing that I was going to be diagnosed with breast cancer. It started as a stage one diagnosis with a lumpectomy and soon became stage three with lymph node involvement and a mastectomy of my left breast. Feeling into my body I knew the cancer had progressed. The course recommended was chemotherapy and radiation. I was in fear and was looking outside myself to be saved. Those around me were in fear also having lost other loved ones to cancer. I embarked on the treatment suggested by my oncologist and was very quickly fighting for my life. Now I knew the seriousness of this time and that a strong inner stance was needed. It brought me back to myself, to a knowing of who I truly was. I called on my angels, my guides, my Christed self, all I knew to be supporting me in the higher realms and worlds began opening. The veils between this world and other realms began opening up for extended periods of time. Up until this point I had had moments of connection and knowing but I would push them away with my busy life. Now all I had was time to be, to rest, to regenerate. My grandmother, who had passed, would come to visit me in the night. My connection to my inner self was budding, being nourished in the quiet of the days and nights, and I began to open my heart to my deeper knowing within. There were days I didn't think I would make it through to the next and I would feel my life force waning. There were days when the pain was so excruciating I didn't want to make it to the next day. After a very long two years of needles, drugs, surgeries and hospitals, I was declared in remission.

One would think that after this experience I would be well on my way to living a very different kind of life, not resembling the life lived previously. My marriage was crumbling and I was realizing he was not my soul mate. The spiritual school I was associated with was no longer in resonance with me and I was giving my power away all the time. My work as an art therapist in a hospital was the last place I wanted to be. So what did I do? I dug even deeper into my marriage and my role as a spiritual teacher. I did change my career and started ElderArts-an art therapy program working with those in the ending years of life. I was going to be more committed, more giving, and more "in control." That was it, the C word for me was control; Control=Cancer. My life force was going into trying to control everything within me and outside of me. My life had become all about controlling again. Faster, harder, round I went, working constantly and furiously, becoming more and more exhausted. I finally fell onto my couch utterly exhausted late one afternoon in 2009 and had an epiphany. My higher self made it clear that I could go on existing like this but I would be spiritually dead. I would become the walking dead. In that moment I felt the truth of it. I woke up and my life began to change rapidly. Within several months I left the spiritual school and began to connect to the spirit within me. Letting myself be guided from within through my higher guidance system. No longer would I look outside or to another for answers. I was beginning to sit in myself and look within. I began meditating on a daily basis and started attending Alanon as a spiritual guidance system based on the wisdom of my higher self. I was again coming home to my inner knowing. I was beginning to sit within myself and be.

I was changing rapidly within and my outer world was reflecting this. Everything began to speed up. My younger sister, Tara, was diagnosed with stage four colon cancer and I was committed to helping her in any way possible. We set a trip to John of God in Brazil for healing. I quit my all-consuming jobs. I sold our home and separated then divorced my husband. I started a sculpture residency in Vermont for two months. I began to travel to sacred sights, hiking and painting what was coming through. I traveled down the Grand Canyon on a raft painting for eight days, sleeping at night in nature. I ventured around the globe to experience different sacred gatherings to which I was called. I began, for the first time in my life, to open to my true nature and to fall in love with myself. Now I was ready to embark on a deeper journey within my sacred self!

I was called to move to TX after my sister's passing in 2012 to be closer to her family and to my mother. I knew this would not be a permanent move and promised myself while I was living there I would commit to myself and my art. I would not distract myself in the many different ways I had previously done. I found I could no longer live in a big city and bought a home in the country. This small farming/ranching town of 300 people was calling me home to myself. I set up a painting studio and a welding shop. I was literally on fire with sculpting as I began to repurpose metal pipes into different forms of lighting. I was using the fire to open up the metal-to crack it open to the light. What I see now is I was mirroring what was happening within me—I was being cracked open to the brilliant light within. My lighting/sculpture was going into galleries in the Houston/Austin areas and I was now being paid for doing what I absolutely loved.

It had been almost two years of being with and for my divine self. For the first time in my life, I was not trying to escape my true nature. I was curious and wanted more of Me. It was a time of many different feelings and thoughts as I was purging so much. I started getting very tired and then one morning I woke up with welts appearing on my neck. I was so tired, I would be in bed for a day and then could function for a few days and then it was back to bed for a day. I did not want to rush off to a doctor as I was trying to find the answers from within. Then, after a few days of a high fever, I made an appointment and the diagnosis was I possibly had tuberculosis. They said there was shadowing in my lungs and they wanted to watch me for a week. The welts continued to grow on my body and now moved onto my legs. I finally became so sick, a friend said she was taking me to the emergency room. So to Houston I went and they admitted me to the hospital. After three inconclusive days of one doctor's diagnosis being an autoimmune disease they had no name for and another doctor convinced it was lung cancer, I checked myself out of the hospital. I went back home and went within. I had a trip planned to the beach in Maine where I was staying for a month. I decided I would stop over in Boston and make an appointment with my oncologist from previous years. The appointment was full of biopsies of the welts now covering my legs. With every cut into my leg, my body reeled. The trauma of the past experiences screaming out, "no, not again." Again nothing was conclusive. My bloodwork was fine; however, they were concerned with what they were calling black glass in my lungs. They wanted to do a lung biopsy, which meant going back into the hospital. My whole self shouted to go to the beach and schedule the biopsy for the following month, which is what I did. My energy was still very low but I drove to Maine and found my place on the beach. Friends of mine nearby had brought over some books and did Reiki sessions. I was in bed, not able to do much but I would walk the beach. I started reading a book on the practice of Ho'oponpono and started walking the beach in a Ho'oponpono meditation.

And now I was at the spot again where the outside world was telling me cancer was showing up again. How was I going to respond now? I had a deep inner knowing that my body knew how to heal itself and it will guide me in how to do this. I was here, showing up for myself and not in fear. I could heal myself. So every day my body guided me. I was guided to cleanse my body by juicing, which I did for over a month. Every morning I would begin with meditation and Reiki healing as my body guided. My body started toning and moving energy in ways I had never experienced before. Then I would do a watercolor painting with my eyes closed for the first five minutes and complete it with eyes open sensing the colors that were chosen and the energetic pattern being created. In the afternoon I would walk the beach in my Ho'oponpono meditation. The beautiful loving forgiveness was washing over me. The welts disappeared, my energy came back and I was healed within six weeks. I did not know then but I was healing with the energy of color, light and sound which is now part of my everyday life practice.

As I awakened more and more to the true nature I AM, my channel opened wider and I realized my paintings were energetic transmissions of the different Divine Beings I was channelling such as Mary Magdalene and the Magdalene Collective, Mother Mary, Gaia, Divine Mother Creator and the SophiaChrist Collective. My I Am presence is a direct channel of the Divine Scared Heart I Am. I began expressing this through paintings, poetry and divine written and spoken channels. The light was now pouring through the open space of me.

In June 2012, I ventured to Mt. Shasta. I wanted to visit several sites including that of the sacred red and white springs. The night I arrived I found myself waking late into the night to Mother Mary and an activation of the Rose. The rose has been with me my whole life in many different ways and now the imprint was living within me. The following day I ventured to the springs only to find the grounds now privately owned and closed to the public. As Spirit guided me, I miraculously found my way in and down to the waters. I was told to stand in the waters and immediately started toning and channeling. Then I was guided to take pictures. After forty or so minutes I was guided to leave and I then continued my time on Mt. Shasta. When I returned to Cambridge several weeks later, I sat down to look at the photos I had taken. The pictures of the spring jumped out. The water of the springs was golden and it started to speak. It said that it is the living water of the liquid gold plasma light and it is here to nourish and increase the golden light within each of us. It is here to help usher in the golden age by mirroring the golden light within each of us. I was instructed to print out copies of it and put them around my house. When I enlarged the photo I began to see the different beings and portals in the water and then noticed that they continued to change. It truly was a living light water portal. Within several months I was instructed to create a lightbox of this water and to sit within it and meditate. So following my instructions from Source Self I designed and built what I called the liquid gold plasma lightbox and proceeded to sit in it every morning while I meditated. Every time I would go into the space it felt as if I were finally home in myself. I felt the Divine Feminine and Divine Masculine merging as One and uniting in Sacred Union within me. It began to permeate my cells with its golden light and to inform and mirror this golden light to the golden light of my DNA. I felt nourished and loved, seen and held, empowered with the reflection of my golden self. As I sat day after day, I found myself sitting more deeply in my sovereign I Am presence and opening further to the Oneness. After many months of sitting in the golden light water, I ventured to Glastonbury, England. It is the sister sight of the red and white springs in Mt. Shasta. There, in the Divine Feminine red spring and the Divine Masculine white spring, the union of the two became one in me and birthed the Traveling Oracle of the Temple of Light. This is where I Am at present as I write from the road on my journey with the Temple of Light.

I Am the Energy of the Sacred Diamond Heart
The Divine Feminine of this Earth Plane
I Am the Diamond Beauty Way
Open to the Rose of Your Heart
And Radiate Your Love!

ABOUT KATHLEEN QUIGLEY

Kathleen is a visual artist and channel of the Divine I AM presence. The liquid plasma light water experiences are immersions into the Temple of Light where you experience that which is coming forth from your beloved Creator Self. Her Oracle Elements card deck provides an in-depth reading of all that is coming forth.

Kathleen's life experience includes a B.A. in Art and an M.A. in Art Therapy.

Her younger years were spent as a visual artist; furniture maker, painter and sculptor. She created the Art Therapy program at Children's Hospital Boston and Elderarts. She believes that creativity is the forgotten language of the heart. She is on a mission to empower us back into our true blueprint-that of Creator.

Kathleen hosts living experiences using different liquid plasma light waters in color, sound, and light experiences for groups and individuals. She also holds individual sessions through Zoom.

Website: www.kathleenquigley.com
Email: kathleenquigleyart@gmail.com

18

KIMBERLEY JONES

EXCERPTS FROM EAST WITHIN WEST

The worn spots on the green upholstered seats of the city bus looked like splatter from a spilled bottle of calligraphy ink. Most of the city buses in Taipei were built in the 1950s and were still being used in 1969. Nine-year-old Tian Guo was perched on top of one of these seats to make sure he didn't miss getting off at the right stop. Out the window, he could see Yangming mountain rise out of the haze of tropical heat weighing down on the Taipei metropolis.

Taipei bustled with modern stores alongside traditional Chinese medicine shops. Makeshift food vendors on every second corner hawked fresh chicken livers, octopus tentacles and stomach stripe. Tian Guo's mouth watered at the sight of the dim sum stalls selling BBQ pork bao and sticky rice cakes filled with sweet red bean paste. As the bus left the city limits, the scenery changed to traditional Chinese stores owned by independents. No brand names or box stores out here. With less pollution, the air started to smell cleaner. The food vendors were far less frequent as it was difficult to perch a small Bunsen burner on a hillside. Restaurants with outdoor patios and stupendous views of Yangmingshan were more common. They had the added bonus of serving renowned local dishes.

In the early morning that day, Tian Guo's orders were straightforward. "Go get Grandma," his mother, Lin Yu-kuei had barked at him. Tian Guo looked forward to the hour-and-a-half-long ride to fetch Grandma who lived up in the mountains just outside of Taipei city. It was one of the few times he could be by himself outside of the one-room apartment where his two younger sisters, father, and mother lived.

He remembered the stop well. A few meters before the stop, he pulled the stop request cord. The driver looked up and wondered how a little boy could be so independent as to ride a bus for so long all by himself.

"Have a good day."

"You too, mister."

A short walk past the bus stop, Tian Guo walked down a narrow lane that was overgrown with ratty-looking hibiscus and birds of paradise plants. These were considered weeds in Taiwan. When he turned into his destination, a small hut appeared before him. The front door was fastened with barely one hinge as the other one was half broken. He yelled out, "Wai-po (mother's mother), I'm here. Mama wants you to come quickly. I have another sister now."

The old woman sat dozing in one of the two chairs in the hut. The only other piece of furniture was the makeshift bed made out of a piece of plywood set atop concrete blocks with a thin mattress and holey blankets on top of it. She stirred from her slumber only when she heard the word 'sister.' Wai-po thought: *Good golly, what has that crazy daughter of mine done now? Can't she zip up her vagina? I'm gonna give her a good talking to this time.* The front door flew open.

"Sun-zi (grandson)! You woke me up! Bring me some oolong tea."

Tian Guo ran past his wai-po and almost tripped on the small carpet under her feet. Its pattern was so faded that it was impossible to distinguish what the original colours were. He entered the 'kitchen,' an area of about three by four feet that contained two cupboards, a counter, a sink and a rickety table upon which the single cooking element rested. He bent down under the table to turn on the gas from the cylinder resting on the floor. A hissing sound came out, as well as the smell of residual natural gas. The element was turned on and a pot of water began to heat up. Tian Guo measured the tea leaves in the exact amount Wai-po liked and dumped them into the cleanest mug he could find, which had about thirty years of tea stains in it.

"Can you hurry, Wai-po?"

"Don't rush me! Can't you see I'm old? You're not going blind at the age of nine already, are you?

"No, of course not. But I promised Mama I'd bring you back before the baby wakes up from her nap."

"What does that mother of yours think I am? An on-call nanny she can summon at any moment her heart desires?"

Wai-po drank her tea slowly. Tian Guo was used to being patient with her, but today he forgot to bring enough patience.

"Are you almost done with your tea, Wai-po?"

Her right hand flung out as if to slap his face, but he was quick like a cheetah and narrowly avoided the swipe.

Finally, she was done with the tea. Wai-po insisted Tian Guo take her arm in his to escort her to the bus stop. After waiting what seemed an eternity, the bus finally came and off they went, back home to where the new baby was.

"Lin Yu-kuei! What have you done? You know full well you and your laogong (husband) cannot possibly afford to feed another mouth! You had to give up Su-fang when she was already a toddler. She hung on to that Canadian woman's leg like she was going to provide her very last meal. The Canadian couple even gave her an English name immediately after the adoption. She is Kim now! Su-fang is no longer yours. You'll never see her again. Stop trying to replace her!"

Lin Yu-kuei started to sob, which crescendoed to a wailing pitch. Her mother continued the verbal abuse over the sounds of her daughter's grief.

"You better be giving up Su-mei! Look, you can't even look after her. Tian Guo changes her diapers, just like he did with Su-fang. Tian Guo feeds her. Tian Guo plays with her. Tian Guo takes her out into the sunshine. Tian Guo is not the baby's parent. You are!"

The tiny apartment filled up with more sobs from Lin Yu-kuei.

Wai-po finally relented and allowed her daughter to recover her composure.

Chi-Kun arrived home from the army base where he was paid a pittance for being a good soldier in Chang Kai-Shek's army. He walked past his taitai (wife) and his mother-in-law, knowing that nothing good could come out of interfering in their tenuous relationship. He kissed the baby's forehead and then asked Tian Guo if he had changed the diaper recently. The baby stank.

As the months wore on, it was clear the Zhengs could not afford to raise Su-mei as Chi-Kun's meager army salary barely kept his wife, three older children and himself fed and clothed. He realized now it had been a mistake to keep me for so long past my baby stage until they decided to give me up for adoption at the fully grown age of three and a half years old. He wasn't about to make the same mistake twice. He reiterated to his taitai that before she became too attached to Su-mei, he was going to contact Charlie Tao and see if he could find an able family for Su-mei, just like he did for me. Sure enough, nine months after Su-Mei was born (in March 1970), Chi-Kun contacted the same policeman in the Taipei Police Force who worked with my Canadian father and asked for his assistance in finding adoptive parents for his baby daughter once again. Charlie Tao reached out to my father who turned to his wife, Ainslie. She belonged to the American Women's Association (AWA), a social group organized by the wives of expats living in Hong Kong. Ainslie relayed Charlie Tao's message to the AWA who contacted the future adopted mom of Su-mei, Gladys Baxter. The Baxters gave an American name—Alicia—to Su-mei. (How unbelievable that both our adopted moms happened to know each other as members of the AWA in the same year.)

Gladys and Jimmy Baxter seemed like the ideal couple to adopt Su-mei. They were young—only twenty-five and twenty-eight years old respectively. The couple was recently married, so they were still in their honeymoon phase. Jimmy had a steady paying job in the US Air Force and was finishing his posting in Hong Kong right around the time of adopting Su-mei. He and Gladys came back home to Texas to raise their newfound daughter, who they named Alicia.

~

In 2001, I found my birth family still living in Taipei, Taiwan, through two weeks of emails to the Taipei office of the Pearl Buck Foundation and a government department that kept track of all twelve addresses my birth family had lived at from when I was adopted in 1968 to 2001. After the initial happy shock of finally meeting someone who looked like me for the first in thirty-seven years, my birth mother shuffled a bunch of papers in her hands. Then, she handed me a worn-out photo of a young mom dressed like Marlo Thomas from That Girl and a photocopy of my birth sister's adoption papers, written only in Chinese. Through a translator, my birth mother explained:

"Your mama, brothers and sisters would like you to search for this youngest daughter of their family. Due to their complete lack of English, no one in the family feels they would be able to locate her in the United States. Since you're fluent in English, presumably, you'll have a better chance of finding Su-mei."

Mama handed the remaining bunch of papers to me, which included a letter written in Chinese, but with the names of the American couple (Gladys and James Baxter) in English and their last known address in the United States in 1970, which was an APO (Army Post Office/US Military) address. The baby's birth date and date of adoption were also written in this letter.

Since there wasn't much information, I felt like this was a daunting task. I told my birth family I'd do my best.

I felt an overwhelming duty to search for my 'American' sister since it was obvious none of my birth siblings stood a chance due to their language barriers. I was also eager to have a conversation with a birth sibling who could speak English fluently. As soon as I returned home to Canada, I started the search that lasted twelve long years. Finally, the birth and adoption dates on the letter proved to be the most useful information in eventually finding this elusive sister.

In the summer of 2013, I took a vacation to California to visit friends and relatives, and to further the search for my younger birth sister. The last known address I had for her adoptive parents was in

California. I visited a Social Security office in Oakland and discovered Gladys Baxter had passed away in 2007. No wonder I had no luck finding James Baxter when I first started the search in 2001—I had assumed Alicia's parents were still alive. I then searched obituary websites and found Gladys Baxter on a people search website. The site listed only one relative to Gladys, named Alicia. I searched a bit further and found four Alicia Baxters. My heart skipped a beat when I found the Alicia Baxter whose birth date matched that of my younger birth sister. I turned to Facebook and found that same Alicia. She had posted current pictures of herself as well as two pictures of herself when she was probably about four or five years old. The little girl struck me immediately as having a familial resemblance to myself and our birth family. With excitement beyond belief, I shouted to myself, "I found her!" After twelve long years, I finally found my younger birth sister.

On our first phone conversation, we chatted for more than three hours.

"What was your adoptive family like?" I asked.

"Oh, that's a long story. I could write a book about them."

She launched into her past: she told me about her abusive mother, including the incident when she came home five minutes late one night in high school. She told the counselor at school about the beating, and they called the police, which just made things worst for her at home. She told me that from an early age, she knew that she didn't deserve the abuse, and didn't seek out abusive romantic relationships. She had an ex-husband, Eric, who didn't treat her badly but was never in love with her. I shifted in my chair as my mind was racing a million miles a minute. This was a lot to comprehend in one conversation, especially since it was our very first one. I immediately felt sorry for Alicia, but she seemed to know when to get out of abusive situations so, at the time, I admired her. She seemed really happy that I found her. While I tried not to have any expectations about finding any of my birth family members, now I could see why so many adoptees are so hesitant to look for long-lost relatives. It isn't just rejection that is at the forefront of our minds but it's the fear of the complete unknown as to what lives those family members have lived through and how their trials and tribulations have shaped their personalities. After all, birth family members are still essentially strangers whom an adoptee has to get to know and establish relationships with, just like all other human beings do with new coworkers or friends on a regular basis. The only things birth families and adoptees have in common are DNA and familial resemblances, which become meaningless if our personalities don't really jive.

I was amazed at how she survived so much physical and verbal abuse. I asked her if she was able to turn to her father. She explained that her mother made it difficult for her to see her father since she hated him so much for all the cheating. Gladys wouldn't allow Alicia to see him after her parents divorced. She launched into another story: "My father and I arranged meetings in secret, and he remarried shortly after the divorce. My father had twin sons with his second wife, who are fifteen years younger than me. They suffered a horrific event—one was raped on the way home from school one day—and they never emotionally recovered. So, both brothers have lived on welfare all their lives. At one point, a few years ago, I tried to help the brother who was raped by allowing him to live with me (he was homeless at the time). I paid for thousands of dollars of dental work because his teeth were in such bad shape. After all that effort, he decided he wanted to go back to living on the streets, and he left."

I was beginning to wonder if anything had gone right in this girl's life. But it was just a bit crazy that we had lived through somewhat similar traumas. I described the brothers from my adopted family:

"My brothers have lived on welfare all their lives. They never recovered from my father's verbal abuse. I guess I was lucky in some ways because our father only started abusing me when our mother died, but he abused his two sons practically from birth. My brothers are nine and 11 years older than me but one died from alcoholism in 2008, so I just have one brother now, who is still a severe alcoholic. I hadn't talked to him in over nineteen years, but when our father finally died in 2011, we had to reconnect to decide some matters over our father's estate. As it turns out, we actually have a nice relationship now. He still drinks but I try not to let that bother me. He is entitled to live his life the way he sees fit and he's never harmed anyone else due to his drinking, as far as I know, so I realized I shouldn't judge him based on his addiction.

～

I flew down to North Carolina to meet Alicia for the first time, and then, a few months later, we arranged a trip for us to travel together to Taiwan so Alicia could finally meet our birth mother. This was a momentous occasion for the rest of the birth family, and everyone came to greet Alicia and me at the airport. Even though Alicia had never learned Mandarin, she certainly expressed her joy at meeting so many people with whom she shared DNA. There is a historic photo from our first night in Taipei with our birth mother and all our birth siblings together in the lobby of the hotel. It was the first and only time in her entire seventy-five-year life that our birth mother had all six children with her. While most of our siblings didn't speak English, our youngest birth brother, Tian Min, spoke a smattering of English that allowed us to have some communication with our birth family.

After the excitement of reconnecting family members who were broken up over forty-five years ago, Tian Min said to me, "We want to thank you for finding Su-mei. Mama is very happy. Tian Guo wants me to tell you, thank you for bringing the family back together again." I was relieved I succeeded in fulfilling my duty to Mama. Everyone could see how Mama was affected. She couldn't stop smiling.

ABOUT KIMBERLEY JONES

From an impoverished Taiwanese family with too many mouths to feed, Kim was adopted just shy of her fourth birthday to a Canadian couple and thus lived as the only non-Caucasian in an all-white family and was raised in a completely Western culture. Kim's memoir, *East Within West*, is about adoption and surviving the death of the mother who raised her at an early age. Subsequently, over a few decades, Kim was egged on by many friends to write her life story. She started attending creative writing classes at the University of Toronto a few years after she wrote the first chapter. Armed with loads of loving encouragement from the U of T creative writing instructors as well as from her writing classmates, Kim was able to write more chapters. During the pandemic of 2020 - 2021, Kim used the downtime to finally finish the book. She works as an accountant in Toronto, Canada.

May this book inspire others who have grown up in dysfunctional families to have faith in themselves so they too can survive multiple traumas. And hope that tomorrow will bring a brighter day for we can all become whole, kind and empathetic human beings. Each of us matters.

My memoir: www.amazon.ca/dp/B09TG2X72P

19

LEIGH ELLIOTT-DAVIES

LIFE EXPERIENCES AND FINDING MY SPARKLE!

When I was younger, I had a recurring dream of long sandy beaches and turquoise-colored seas. I knew one day I would be living in another country. Little did I know the journey to that destination would be paved in lessons!

I was brought up in a small village, Ystrad Mynach in Wales, to a working-class family. My dad was a miner, and Mam worked in the school canteen. They were very much in love with a passion for enjoying life. The middle child of three girls, I enjoyed camping holidays by the seaside. My parents would always try and give us new experiences along this journey we call life! I was quite a shy child, lacked confidence, hated public speaking and words never came easy. As a child, I loved all things sporty. At age fourteen, I had an ice-skating accident that damaged my knee, requiring months of rehabilitation.

OUT OF INJURY GOOD CAN COME!

Finally, I knew what career path I wished to pursue! I loved helping people and Physiotherapy seemed the best choice. I was lazy at school, just loved sport, and would leave things till the last minute to study and scrape a pass. The requirement to become a Physiotherapist was three A levels, A/B grades!! My thoughts, too much study for me! I found an alternative, join the Army, they train you without A Levels! I informed my dad! In his wisdom, he booked a Youths Adventure Training scheme, in Scotland. I was sixteen years of age and very naïve. My dad left me at the train station in Ystrad, your first task is to find your way to Inverness in Scotland!

FEEL THE FEAR AND DO IT ANYWAY!

After two weeks of experiencing Army Life. Early morning rising at the crack of dawn, being told what to do, survival camps in wet damp forests, catching, skinning a rabbit, and being told to eat it! Climbing Ben Nevis with rocks in your rug sack!! Dad asked, "So you are joining the forces?" You can guess what's coming! I done my A levels!

LIFE ISN'T EASY, GET OUT OF YOUR COMFORT ZONE AND TAKE ACTION!

I studied hard, completed A levels, and qualified as a Physiotherapist in October 1987. I travelled to Spain, Morocco, Portugal and around the Greek Islands finding a passion for travelling! I accepted a job offer in Toronto, Canada. The red tape to attain the necessary paperwork took too long, and my itchy feet wouldn't wait, turning my attention to Australia. I attained a holiday working visa and started planning. Six months before leaving I met the man of my dreams! I knew if I didn't travel as planned, I would regret it! After experiencing a previous breakdown in a relationship, my thoughts, if he's the one he will be there when I return!

GOOD THINGS COME TO THOSE THAT WAIT!

My three-month relationship with Mark was blossoming. The thought of travelling on my own was quite daunting but I knew I could do it. After a beautiful evening, a walk in the park, Mark got down on one knee and proposed! My reactive thoughts were, this is happening all too quickly, what about my travel plans! I declined the proposal stating, "Why don't you ask me when I return from Australia" How insensitive was I!! Mark shrugged it off and hatched a plan to travel to Australia. Three days before leaving one of my best friends was getting married on the grounds of Knebworth House, London. The night before the wedding, Mark appeared on edge, not his usual self. In the Church and outside, whilst our friends were having their photos taken, he was becoming even more restless. He was trying to get my attention and well, he got it! He got down on one knee, produced the ring and asked me to marry him. I instinctively said "yes." The bride and groom shouted over did you say yes? Everyone knew he was going to propose for the second time. Three days later I flew out to Australia as planned. An emotional farewell at the airport, but I knew he would be by my side again soon!

WHEN THE TIME IS RIGHT YOU JUST KNOW WITHOUT HESITATION!

Mark and I travelled around Australia for a year, experiencing some amazing things. Wonderful memories I hold close to my heart. Back home in Wales, it was great catching up with everyone and returning to work as a Physiotherapist, which I loved. However, I yearned to emigrate! Mark had chosen his career path to become a children's nurse, so with plans to emigrate on hold, we focused on our wedding. Mark and I come from very large families; the invite list was 250 guests! In Cardiff, in a travel shop window were pictures of weddings in the Caribbean! You guessed it; we booked it there and then, to elope in the Caribbean and have a massive celebratory party on our return. I think our parents accepted our decision well. My parents had experienced my eldest sister getting married in our local Church. The wedding day was amazing but the preparations, planning and stress leading up to the day were not something I wished for. Just before leaving to get married, good friends decided to come and celebrate with us, so we were blessed with a best man and matron of honor! On 28/09/1993 Mark and I got married in St Lucia in the Caribbean. The wedding and our honeymoon were truly amazing. I remember having to pinch myself, I got to wear my wedding dress twice, at the wedding party on our return.

LIFE CAN TRULY BE BREATHTAKING!

Mark and I hadn't talked about having children. After spending time with our two nieces on a family holiday to Rhodes we decided a family was on the horizon! We planned one last holiday backpacking around Thailand. We had wonderful neighbors where we lived, enjoyed many parties, eating, drinking, and having fun! After a night with our neighbors and too much red wine, I fell pregnant. Everyone had an opinion we should cancel the holiday! With Dr's approval, it's safe to travel, Mark and I enjoyed our last holiday in Thailand before the pitter-patter of tiny feet. Choosing to live it up in hotels rather than backpacking!

FLEXIBILITY IS KEY!

I was nauseous the whole nine months, totally off my food but knew I had to eat to nourish my baby. Josie arrived in March 1997. The delivery was fast. Having practiced meditation/visualization techniques I sailed through it! With the help of a maternity TEN's machine, and no pain medications. It can be done! My maternal instincts fell into place. I was determined to breastfeed! Josie struggled with this, losing weight and I, with sleepless nights, constantly feeding. I was referred to a breastfeeding specialist, learning there is a technique to breastfeeding! I gave in and introduced her to the bottle. She slept through the night, and I did. I regained some normality;

everyone was happy. Sometimes the best intentions are just not meant to be.

LET GO OF YOUR IDEA OF HOW THINGS SHOULD BE AND GO WITH THE FLOW, DOWNSTREAM!

Life was great, then uncomfortable! I fell pregnant with my second child and my sister Susan was diagnosed with breast cancer on 02/09/1998. I remember being positive, there are so many advances in cancer research, people survive all the time, you've got this sis! I remember the fear in her eyes! One year prior to her diagnosis a lump was discovered during a routine check. At thirty-four she had an ultrasound. They didn't do mammograms in patients under thirty-five years of age.

I recall her telling me they didn't scan the right area! I reassured her they're professionals and know what they're doing! Susan developed an odd pain in her thoracic spine and her left arm. As a physiotherapist "Red Flags" were flying. After a mammogram, the diagnosis was finalized. Susan underwent a lumpectomy, radiotherapy and chemotherapy, six months of hell and informed us she had the all-clear! I was seven months pregnant at this stage and instinctively knew this was not the case! Susan was admitted to St Ann's Hospice, Newport, for pain management!

She was in a tremendous amount of pain, on morphine, hallucinating and her breathing had changed. Looking back, I knew Susan was trying to protect us all from the awful news that she had a rapidly progressive form of cancer. There was no cure. She was transferred to The Royal Gwent Hospital, her breathing labored; I knew she was dying. I checked her notes and saw the dreaded NFR!!

Not for resuscitation! I tried to remain calm, composed, but inside I was crumbling. Saying farewell to my sister, we cwtched! I said, "you've got this" She smiled, looked at peace, the fear had gone, even though she was struggling to breathe. She knew I knew. She whispered back "you've got this" I smiled back and left. In the lift, I burst into uncontrollable tears. She took her last breath around 8 pm on

01/04/1999, six months after being diagnosed! My family's life was shattered that day, the sky had tumbled in on our cozy life and things would never be the same again

LIFE CAN BE SO CRUEL!

Timothy was born in June 1999, bringing some joy back into my parents' life. They had always been such positive people but sadly negativity reared its ugly head. They put on a brave face and being retired they maintained their love of dancing, caravanning, and raising money for charities. My dad found some peace whilst gardening and in his allotments. They carried the loss in their hearts, it showed in their eyes. I fell pregnant in June 2001. In my first trimester, after being in contact with a patient with chicken pox, I was given a vaccination to protect my fetus. I needed to isolate for twenty-eight days as it was a live vaccine. The day after the vaccination I noted my stomach had swollen. I couldn't get my jeans on; I was losing blood! My twelve-week scan was postponed until I was out of isolation. At sixteen weeks I was diagnosed with a blighted ovum. There was no heartbeat. I was devastated then suddenly thought of others who didn't have any children, this eased my pain. I was already blessed with two beautiful kids.

THERE IS ALWAYS SOMEONE DOING IT TOUGHER THAN YOURSELF!

I was blessed with a third child, Emma, in March 2003. Time was running out on our plans to emigrate, due to the visa process and my age. Families were informed we're moving to Australia for a couple of years to experience living in another country with our children. Mark's parents, younger than mine, and our extended families thought it was a wonderful opportunity. My parents, who had always supported me in everything I had done, just threw all the negatives at me! They were close to their grandchildren and saw it as another loss. They could visit and experience Australia, but Dad was adamant he would never travel. Did my parents just need time to adjust to the idea?

This was a very difficult time for me. This little 'bluebird of happiness' fell off its perch, over the cliff into the deepest black hole you can imagine! No one can truly understand anxiety and depression unless you experience it yourself! I was diagnosed with an acute anxiety state. I was struggling to eat, felt constant nausea, and all my thoughts were negative, very dark. I lost weight, couldn't sleep and my brain wasn't functioning. I tried medication and became suicidal! I just couldn't live in that black hole, struggling to see the light. I recall the pitter-patter of tiny feet on the floorboards in the morning, would hide under the duvet so the kids couldn't see me like this.

My husband took them to school, and I read the same sentence from a book repeatedly until I heard him return. Fearful I would go downstairs and kill myself. I became agoraphobic and couldn't leave the house. I knew my thoughts were totally irrational but was struggling to control them. My every thought was so negative, I was scrambling in the dark and couldn't see a way out.

I turned to Acupuncture. It worked and with previous life experiences, and age, I was able to rationalize my thoughts and see the light! Family and friends' support made it easier for me. Three months later I was able to venture out into the world again, and I felt back in some sort of control! When you hit rock bottom, you must rise, find inner strength and fight for your life.

THIS GAVE ME INSIGHT INTO WHY PEOPLE SADLY COMMIT SUICIDE!

I emigrated to Perth, Australia, in March 2006! Things didn't go smoothly. Three days before leaving our house sale fell through! With very little money, three kids in tow, we arrived in Australia. I had contacted the Australian Physiotherapy Association and been informed I could get a visa to work immediately as I had worked in Australia before. This information was incorrect, I had to go through the process of presenting my papers, sitting an exam, and completing three practical exams! This took time and a whole lot of money. Mark was able to work immediately, nursing. Episodes of anxiety reared their ugly head! Mark and I argued a lot, which we had never done before, over our financial situation. I was stuck in a poverty mindset and had developed further unhealthy habits around money. I struggled to spend money, hated any type of shopping. Gaining my registration was a nightmare but I did it. In August 2012, I landed my first job working in a private practice! Yes, it took six years!

PERSISTENCE IS KEY, NEVER EVER GIVE UP!

The turning point came in September 2013. I felt exhausted, on a treadmill in life, on the road to nowhere! Money coming in, money going out, struggling to survive, and not LIVING! I came across a company that was changing people's lives and took a leap of faith. Fueled with the best nutrition I started to feel a million dollars! After just one month I felt ALIVE for the first time in ages. The energy levels I had before kids had returned, the fog had lifted, I could think clearly again. As a side effect, I achieved my ideal weight! The increased energy levels gave me back my passion for life! I now run my own business "Home Physiotherapy Solutions" Promoting health and wellbeing in the community. This had been a dream of mine for many years. I truly believe had I not discovered the gift of Isagenix I would not have had the confidence, drive, or energy to achieve my dream.

GOOD NUTRITION AND HEALTH ARE EVERYTHING!

Along with Isagenix came a community of like-minded people and the world of self-development! I attended courses and read all the right books. I had awakened and was seeing things I hadn't seen before. I now understand the power of now, living in the present moment! I discovered the "Magic of the Universe and the law of attraction." Well, I just had to put this to the test! I wished to attend Celebrations in Brisbane in March 2015 and attend the Gala event.

Financially we couldn't afford it and had three kids to think about. The money arrived for the flight; friends offered to look after the kids. I walked past a shop, saw a ball gown, and purchased it! No more poverty mindset for me! Mark pointed out the Gala event was sold out. I smiled; the universe will provide! Three days before flying, tickets were given to us for the ball.

It was the most amazing experience. I am forever grateful I put trust in the universe! I lost the stone out of my engagement ring. My late sister helped Mark purchase the ring, I loved it! I retraced my steps that day, searched bins, my handbag, the car, the pavements... and couldn't find it. It was like trying to find a needle in a haystack. Every day for three months I was looking for that stone and guess what, it appeared! I was getting rid of an old handbag I had previously searched in. I emptied the contents onto the table, the lining fell out, embedded in the lining was something shining, my stone! My ring has returned to its former glory. It's all about the energy in the universe and vibrating at the right frequency.

MIRACLES CAN HAPPEN IF YOU BELIEVE!

The Monad Centre in Joondalup was instrumental in my journey, enhancing my meditation skills. I am forever grateful for their wisdom and guidance. An important part in life is keeping your mind, body, and spirit in balance. I am content and at peace with all that I am, I have, and I do. I count my blessings!

I NOW KNOW SELF-LOVE IS KEY!

After reflecting on my life on a recent family holiday to Wales, and soul searching in the Swiss Alps it's time to step up! I need to shine, assist others to find their sparkle, achieving inner peace and happiness. I'm guided to stop holding back, ditch the monkey on my shoulder and impact more lives. Working with gratitude, from my heart of contribution and giving back. I feel like standing on top of the world, sprinkling fairy dust everywhere! I wish to open everyone's minds, who will listen, to the power of living in the present, having an attitude of gratitude and enjoying the law of attraction! Who wouldn't be open to a little magic in their lives! My wish for you! Ditch what no longer serves you, get out of your head and into your heart, embrace the new and experience contentment!

Mark and I have big plans to sell everything, buy a boat in the Mediterranean and sail around the world! I know the universe, God, has my back!

ABOUT LEIGH ELLIOTT-DAVIES

Leigh Elliott-Davies is an entrepreneur and network marketer. Her vision is a life of abundance for everyone, with a passion for inspiring all to find inner peace and contentment in life!

Leigh qualified as a Physiotherapist at The University Hospital of Wales in October 1987, gaining post-graduation qualifications in Acupuncture/dry needling for pain management. Leigh specializes in Musculoskeletal out-patients, sports therapy, aged care, and neurological rehabilitation. Her dedication to promoting the best possible outcome and her holistic approach has assisted countless patients/clients over the years.

In Perth, Leigh launched her business "Home Physiotherapy Solutions" Promoting health and Wellbeing in the community in August 2014.

Family is her joy, inspiring her adult children to live their most fulfilling life. In her spare time, Leigh can be found enjoying music to lift the soul, dancing/exercise/yoga to fire the spirit and meditation/sailing to calm the mind.

Website: *www.vehicle4success.isagenix.com*
Email: *Leigh@homephysiotherapysolutions.com.au*

20

NADINE PARKINSON

Dedicated to the Reader
Thank you for being here, for taking the time to read my chapter.
I hope I leave you touched or inspired to do something out of your comfort
zone. May you rise to the challenges that you face every day and do it with
enthusiasm and a smile! You never know what life has in store for you. Live
your best life now and do the things that make you happy today! In writing
this, I have been privileged to be a student and learn more about myself. In
preparation for this chapter, I shared that it would be unjust for me not to
contribute to this book.
I hope you find something in here for you.

Proverbs 3:5
Arohanui (with love)
Nardz xx

I **have to take a moment to sit and laugh at myself.**
This is my first time writing a chapter for a book, and I
have never been one to write down my thoughts consistently and

stick to the task at hand. My journal writing is sporadic and if anyone was to try and follow me in that area, I wish them nothing but luck. Even I struggle to see where I'm at some days, on and off the paper! Procrastination, avoidance, and resistance at their finest. It's always been easier to let the mind run wild than to sit in the heart space and allow the flow to come through. I will usually let my mind be distracted and if there was a medal, I'm sure I'd be in the running for GOLD! Can I just say for the record, I've checked my phone a dozen times already since the writing of this paragraph (insert palm-to-forehead emoji here)

I have just gotten home from a massage and meditation class, and I'm still challenged for the mind to settle. I am not trying to stop the mind from running away but taking the time to ask my higher self what state I need to be in to write with no limitations.

This is an opportunity for my inner child to be free and explore!

Aha, that's it!!! (there goes my first aha moment for the chapter)

When I ask good questions, I get good answers.

I can only describe it as taking my inner child by the hand and with love, certainty and reassurance, letting her know that this chapter is about sharing, caring, acknowledging, being playful and permission to be in a childlike state. She is excited and any resistance that was previously there has now left the building! BOOM!!!

With a chapter deadline to meet, I can recall many times in my life when I would leave certain and usually important things to the last minute, this is no exception. Exam studying was always left on the "to-do" list the night before the test. However, you give me a travel idea and within minutes I've found the best flight deals and the suitcases are out on the bed, ready for packing. Amazing how quickly we can get into action when we are passionate about something we love to do and leave no room for excuses. I'm not sure if it's the adrenalin or suspension but it actually only serves me high anxiety and lots of unnecessary rewriting, wasted paper and trips more often to my hairdresser for the touch-ups on the greys.

If I can be totally honest with you and myself for that matter, I would say I am a perfectionist. I like things to look and be a certain way. I can only do things if it's perfect, so why start in the first place right??? I have missed a lot of wonderful opportunities and have not seen plans come to fruition because of this perception of perfectionism. I have avoided looking at it also, so when it shows up it's actually more exhausting being in denial. Definitely not my authentic self coming to the party. So the question is, am I really a perfectionist or am I just afraid of failure??? And where in my life have I first experienced this?

That way of thinking and being has not served me for as long as I can remember. If anything, it has caused me a lot of unnecessary heartache and pain and not to mention, the pain inflicted on others.

This is the part where I acknowledge openly that those previous versions of myself are not who I am today. I have grown and learnt a lot about myself since then and it will be an ongoing process of learning.

Part of any healing journey is first acknowledging that there is hurt. For me it's followed by the acceptance that I cannot change what has happened, forgiveness of myself and others, addressing the issue or challenging the belief at hand. Letting go and striving to be and do better towards myself first and then others. How can I help heal others if I haven't healed myself? For me, it's having empathy, compassion, love, self-love and self-awareness. It's showing up when I don't want to, it's letting go of my ego, it's being humble and in service to others, it's staying the course when I can't see the road. It also looks like taking regular moments to check in with oneself. In hindsight, I can now see why I have become so passionately involved in different community groups that serve in contributing to healing.

A friend recently reminded me of the acronym H.A.L.T. Hungry, Angry, Lonely, Tired. When I have been in one or more of these states at one time, I have not shown up as my best self and in the past, it has led to burnout. I can do it, add one more thing to the list, I've got this (when I really hadn't) the not asking for help scenarios all play out and the burnouts had resulted in me being in bed for a minimum of two days.

I would feel like a failure and beat myself up about it.

Nowadays though, I am more self-aware of how I'm feeling and take the necessary steps to address what's there for me earlier rather than later. And as Matt Brown shares in his book *She Is Not Your Rehab*, hurt people, hurt people.

I had been carrying a lot of hurt around for many years and didn't even know it. Like when I was nineteen years old and blamed my doctor for my bad health issues that resulted in a ruptured appendix. I remember being in a pitch-dark room alone with my eyes closed, pleading to stay here on this earth. For some reason, I knew it was going to be one of my last moments if I didn't ask the Divine to intervene. I have only ever cried that hard one other time in my life so I knew this was serious. With the Divine on my side, I managed to push through and survive. I am a survivor. I have known this since my birth and I'm reminded every day especially when I look at my scar from the blotchy surgeries that resulted.

Or the times I would blame my ex-husbands (yes, plural) for not making me happy. When they weren't doing things to my standard or in my timely manner, I would get upset. It was their job to make me happy, wasn't it??? Well, that's what I thought at that time anyway and boy, did I have a lot to learn. I'm more awake and conscious now if that version tries to rear its ugly head. Trust me, it's always a learning process and don't get me wrong, at the end of the day I'm still human and I still make mistakes. This is also an opportunity to apologize to anyone who has ever experienced those not-so-great versions of me, and I ask for your forgiveness.

As I evolve and move through different stages and phases of this life, I learn, adapt, grow and thrive. When I recognise that I am unhappy or not thriving, I know I'm not doing the things that I love. Sometimes it's letting go of something, a job change, an end to a relationship, or a habit that no longer serves me. It is recently looking like an overseas trip to Hawaii for my first marathon! All of these things take courage, time, sacrifice, self-belief and backing myself one hundred per cent of my decision-making. Overcoming the inner dialogue and doing it regardless of any fear that may be holding me back. And TRUST. Trusting myself and what I am doing or about to do is for the greater good of me and humanity. Remembering that we all have something to contribute to this world and as Jay Shetty reminded me in his book, *Think like a Monk*, finding your dharma.

When I share with others what I'm up to in my life, I'm amazed at how many people will give me advice or their opinion on things they have no idea about. I take it humbly and work out for myself if what is being shared is of value to me. If it resonates, it usually comes back around to me in one way or another, or I'll receive a nudge or some form of a reminder that the information is important. One time when I didn't listen to the nudge I ended up with a $400 fine and three demerit points. Just goes to show that if you get prompted, pay attention.

Also, be mindful of people who, especially when you are in your element, may try to pull you down, make negative comments and try to sabotage what you have worked hard for. We will trigger others when we are being our authentic selves; however, take note of when you are being triggered as well and work on it. Utilize it to your advantage and it will serve its purpose. Stay focused and surround yourself with like-minded people and vibe your tribe!

I have learnt that what others have to say about me is none of my business so if there's one thing I can say here it's this, don't get caught up in your small-minded thinking, rise above it. Taking an eagle eyes view of situations helps a lot, it's being able to detach and stop making things mean things in order to progress.

In 2018, I had the opportunity to travel with the New Zealand Influence Crew and completed my first half marathon on the Great Wall of China. That was a huge achievement for me. Not only did I push beyond what I thought I was capable of mentally and physically, but I also went one step further and fundraised all the money to go. I also reached out to small businesses for sponsorship and enrolled others on the conversation about my trip, which in turn, they became my support crew on my social media platform. During the training and lead up to the very last day of my departure, I still questioned if I had done enough training. My mind was trying to deter me from believing I could complete this challenge. However, once out on the marathon course with all the people, the culture and the beautiful surroundings, I found myself in a state of total bliss! There was nothing that could stop me from completing what I had set out to do. To this day, I can still see me and a couple of my close friends crossing that finish line together. With tears in our eyes, we rejoiced together and celebrated our victory! This will be me this coming December as I participate in my first marathon in Hawaii. I have talked about going to this beautiful land for the past ten years and for the record I want to add that I have never seen myself as a runner but more of a slow jogger/walker but always about the mental challenge, participation and accomplishment.

Regardless of the event, it has always been important for me to acknowledge the spiritual realm. Always asking for help, guidance, protection, the right people and experiences and it always shows up perfectly. An example is when I'm asking for a VIP parking bay at the shops, ninety per cent of the time one will appear just for me, even when the lot is full! I believe that where you are right now is where you're meant to be and everything that you experience in life is exactly how it's supposed to be, whether it's good or not so good. This can be hard to understand sometimes, especially when you are going through tough times. I also believe this way of thinking is deep seeded and stems from my Maori culture, our people would karakia (or pray) for and about everything.

At this point, I feel it is important to share about my upbringing, my family and most importantly, my parents.

My mum is from the tribe of Tainui. She was a gorgeous, loving, nurturing woman who raised many kids from a young age. She loved smoking, bingo and cards, which is where my siblings and I get some of our favorite pastimes from. Unfortunately, I can't say I inherited her love of housework. My dad left his tribe of Tuhoe when he was young and rode his motorbike north with a couple of mates to find work. He changed his age so he could enlist for the war and to this day we still laugh about what his real age actually is.

My dad is a tough guy, a real old skool. He taught us kids a lot, especially around table etiquette, manners and living in a western world. He was raised in a time when Maori was his first language and then to attend school and be punished for speaking it. He was an outstanding international rugby league player and represented the New Zealand Kiwi Team of 1964. He still resides in our homestead in Huntly that he built.

Growing up I had low self-esteem and found it challenging to articulate words to express myself. I would get an emotional buildup, which would result in tears and depending on the circumstance or situation, the body is a great indicator of letting me know that I'm still holding onto the unexpressed emotion or I am left incomplete about something. I've always been an empath so letting go or detaching has always been a real challenge. Growing up, I never learnt about things like breathwork, meditation or yoga that would help me shift from this state. Even sitting down, talking and having someone I trust to hold the space for me to express and let go. I would like to hope that from these past experiences I can hold the space for others. Not being in full self-expression has resulted in excessive weight gain, erratic mood swings, withdrawal and even depression. I can't ever recall sitting around the dining table having deep and meaningful conversations about these things. I would also rebel a lot against my parents as a result and not knowing that they were doing their best with what skills they had at that time. In saying all this, I am either at one end of the spectrum or the other. I swing like a pendulum and try to find a middle balance. Because I am conscious of this, it makes the process a lot smoother. Things like walking, talking, listening to great podcasts and motivational speakers and spending time with my family have helped me immensely in this area. I have also come to realise the importance of clean eating, plenty of water, vitamin D and having a positive mindset makes a huge difference. These things help me to make better decisions, build confidence and attract more opportunities.

Our home was one of order, things had to be a certain way. Laundry was always done, washed, dried and ironed. Dinner table set and washing up was always done before any TV was switched on or leaving the house. I have no doubt that's where my perfection perception came from. I'm not sure how the upcoming generation would cope with doing some of these things on a regular basis nowadays.

There were always plenty of parties and card games at home that would usually go on for a couple of days. Drinking and smoking became part of the norm for me, especially in my teens when I would steal cigarettes from my mum's packet, refill the Bacardi bottle on the cabinet with water and spend all my pocket money on going out to do these things.

I remember my mum telling me I could smoke once I got a job, I didn't even know how to write a resume! In sharing, I must say that I did have a wonderful upbringing though, I was very blessed to be part of a huge family where my siblings love me like one of their own (and still do to this day). You will get to read about it when I get around to the full book.

If there's anything I can leave with you, it would be this:

Take time for yourself, do the things you love and if you don't know what that is, go and find out! Overcome and forgive quickly.

I often think of when I leave this earth how I made people feel and how I will be remembered. What legacy do you want to leave??

Be okay with not knowing all the answers. We are all at different competency stages, and if you want something, get off your butt and go get it!

ABOUT NADINE PARKINSON

Nadine Parkinson (a.k.a Nardz) was born and raised in the small Waikato town of Huntly, New Zealand. She is the youngest of eleven children and resides in Perth, Western Australia, where she works as a custody officer.

She shares her personal life experiences through her podcast Living My Best Life and also welcomes women in the business world to add value to the listener's lives through real and raw conversations.

Nardz is passionate about community, culture and connection and volunteers her time with non-profit organization, Haka for Life, a unique platform that raises awareness of suicide prevention and men's mental health.

In 2018 she represented Australia in the world's competition of Waka Ama - Outrigging Canoeing, completed her first half marathon on the Great Wall of China in 2019 and is about to attempt her first Hawaiian marathon this December 2022.

She is the proud Aunty to many beautiful nieces and nephews.

Websites:
www.hakaforlife.org
www.jayshetty.me/podcast
www.sheisnotyourrehab.com/about

21

NICOLETTE WIJERS

THE BOX

The box I never fitted and ... I never will fit...

Growing up in a small village, where everyone knows your name, and worse, think they know your whole story and own your life, I felt out of place from the very beginning.

Being the only child of parents who never got married, a big thing in "town" as that's not what you suppose to do in those times—get engaged, married, buy a house, have babies, Mum looks after the children whilst Dad is the breadwinner—well not in my family and not how my life looked like when I was younger....

We always did things differently, living in a villa in the nicest neighbourhood of town, having everything in life I needed, growing up with many weekends spent outdoors and away on our sailing boat, attending all sports activities and having the best of the best of everything as that was only good enough for me.

But in the background feeling that pressure of always having to perform and be "the best," at school, my speedskating games, playing tennis, doing my homework and anything else I was told how and what to do.

I had the best coach, who trained multiple gold medal Olympic winners, but I was not one of them...

I was very disciplined with my winter training schedule, but I was lacking the motivation to train during the summer and truly push through to the top, as I was out having fun with my friends, much to the disappointment of my dad.

At school I was sitting in the classroom, staring out of the window, daydreaming of all the travel I wanted to do, exploring this big crazy world that was just there to be discovered...

After my graduation, I took off for my gap year to America, where all dreams come true... I went to college to study "hospitality" but instead I partied hard and did all the things you have to discover living on campus with your parents being miles away.....

I had the guts to drive my little car by myself, as a seventeen-year-old, across the country from California to New York City.

I always wanted to be a "world traveller" as my title rather than whatever anyone else had on their name badge... so after meeting my now husband in a bar in Amsterdam (yes, where else do you meet cute Dutch guys?) the first question I asked him on our first date was "What do want to do with your life?" Within months of living together, we planned our trip away. I remember my mum asking me "What if it didn't work out?" Well, I said, "I have my own passport and backpack so that will work out."

So we set sail, on a one-way ticket to Sydney, Australia, no plans, just a single ticket, backpack and each other... we travelled for 2.5 years exploring the world together, having fun, no limitations, no restrictions, no goals only action, no agenda or timeframe, just freedom, exploring, doing all the things our hearts desire, living IN the moment, enjoying life and spending quality time together...

Back home in the Netherlands, we started work again, after experiencing all the freedom the world travelling gave us, we looked at each other and said... "Why are we here? Let's go again"... so we did and this time we moved to New Zealand where we started working in the luxury hospitality industry. The most prestige lodge offered us the huge opportunity of working with celebrities and royalty, so expectations were high, putting pressure on us to perform at the highest level every single day as guests were paying top dollar.

We both worked our way up in search of the ultimate top jobs, which led us to amazing opportunities opening luxury properties all around the world. But I was frustrated, overworked, working 12+ hour days, and I earned much less than I was worth. To make it worse, I never had time to spend with my friends, and I kept missing out on all the fun things in life... because I was always stuck at work building someone else's dreams. It even affected my relationship. I felt more married to my job than to my husband of many years. He did not deserve this!

I felt stuck and undervalued, knowing I deserved more but just didn't know how to get it. Or maybe I DID know...but I was just afraid to take that first step? I was not alone!

I'll never forget the phone call I received... I was living in Asia when I was called for a head office meeting. I'd been asked to come into the office many times before, but this time something felt different... Feelings of fear and uncertainty were bubbling up to the surface and I felt sick to my stomach. When I got to the head office, I was taken to a boardroom, and without any explanation, I was fired for the first time in my life... and get this... for not being "what they are looking for."

In that moment, my heart sank. I had given my all to this company and even sacrificed my personal life. Now, here I was feeling like "I wasn't good enough"...

One thing I realised was that I never wanted to work long hours, be at the mercy of a boss or struggle daily just to build someone else's dreams! At *that* time, I knew what I *didn't* want, but had no idea what I did want...

I was extremely stressed and frustrated, sitting on the couch in our big and beautiful multi-million dollar home, earning the money I could buy what I wanted... but it was the moment when my husband walked into the house after a long day of work, asking me one question:

"What do you *really* want?"... I said, "I just want to be Happy...."

He asked, "how does that look like" and all I could answer was "I don't know" ... as I had no clue what my purpose in life was and where to start....

Although I had everything I wanted, I still felt empty inside myself, the spark in my eyes was gone, I lost all my passion for work, my husband, basically for life. Then, in that moment of pain and disillusion, not just STUCK, but LOST with no direction in life

I was just numb and not even motivated to come off the couch.... But I knew there must be a better way...It's incredible how when you put something out there and you make a decision for change, the universe rearranges itself and brings you exactly what you need.

It wasn't too long after that I was scrolling through my newsfeed coming across a post from a very successful powerful spiritual woman Tamika.

"Find your Soul purpose and the Feminine within You"

I didn't know what it was, but something about those words resonated with me... so I followed my gut feeling to learn more. Before I knew it I found myself sitting in a room full of people who were stuck, not knowing what they wanted in life, the so-called "midlife crisis" ... but I was listening intently as she revealed a proven method of deep inner work releasing all my blocks and what was holding me back to truly live my life to my fullest potential. She had created some powerful education and processes that could help me break free from being unstuck, find my inner self-worth, know who I am and what I'm truly here to do in this world, be a spiritual being living a human life. Listening to my gut feeling, I made my decision very quickly so I jumped all in.

You see, I was an over-thinker, creating lists of pros and cons, before even making a decision, a true procrastinator I was...

This led me to deepen my personal development journey, and to kickstart Awakening my Feminine elevating it in a big way...

She asked me very frequently "How are you Feeling"? and I couldn't give her an answer, as I felt a wave of anger coming over me, I was frustrated and annoyed about her repeatedly asking the same question over and over.... I had to walk out of the room when she asked me again "How are you FEELING?" … This time I said "Nothing" and she answered back "Great…" which made me feel even angrier as I thought she wanted me to give her the right answer…

Learning there is no right or wrong answer, all is good and accepted as that's how I feel in any moment as I move through emotions and feelings all the time, being aware of my triggers and the way I react is what's important so I can take the learnings and implement those into my daily life.

The daily practices I learned about the most important part of healing is the Self Love, which is something I struggled with as I'm a people pleaser and give way more than I will ever receive, but learning the art of Gratitude, Love and Forgiveness has opened my heart to a whole different level I never experienced before. Sitting in a circle with forty other women all being so vulnerable and when sharing my story and the deepest emotions I have never shared with anyone, tears rolling down my cheeks, seeing all women raise their hands, showing respect to what resonates with them, all in different ways, but still the same feeling of "You are not in this alone" and "I'm with you sista" gives a truly deep respect to everyone who is doing "The Work." You need to be brave and courageous to walk this path, but you never walk alone….

"The Art of Surrender & Letting Go" has been one of the toughest ever as I thought I was going to lose everything I had—my house, my car, my career/business, my husband, my family, my friends—but I realized that Having Less is Becoming More, it's not about Things more about Experience and Being.

By finding the networking Queen within me, I connected to a newfound sisterhood. I also found the Love for myself and the deep more meaningful relationship I looked for with my husband. He embarked on a similar journey with the men as his desire to Become a Man was a Journey he needed to go on his own, as a woman can't make a man a man so he had to Run with the Wolves and join the long waited connection with his brotherhood. It showed us although our tram tracks moved in different directions, our values are still aligned after twenty-five years together. Our love has grown stronger, we found a deeper connection and continue our journey as true Soul Mates, experiencing Unconditional Love and not being codependent on each other.

But as I learned many new things, I urge to want more was real... the never-ending temptation and satisfaction kicked in, and my alignment with the "old me" was out of whack so I started to explore new opportunities as they presented themselves...

Understanding that my whole life I have been giving and giving to everyone, but I never took the time and the energy to fill my own cup first again... "How can I pour from an empty cup?" Well, I can't, so I decided to dedicate all my time, energy and money into further education, attending workshops and spending weekends at wellness retreats to dive deep into my own soul healing. Experiencing all the pain and suffering, I felt the urge to truly and deeply heal myself, but realized I had to do this all by myself...

It's a lonely journey as no one else can do this for me, I needed to be courageous and brave as it's not for the faint-hearted to embark on this Journey.... As I had no idea what would happen with and to me ... I needed to take responsibility and only look in the mirror to see there is only ME who can start making that change.

So to get started I had to get the sh...t out of me first before I start putting all the good stuff back into it... remove things out of my life, so I started to detox my body intensely to the core of my being and restoring at cellular levels.

One morning I woke to this incredible pain on the right side of my stomach and after intense research and a visit to the so-called specialist I was told it was my gall bladder and it needed to be removed in case it was cancerous. I asked, "What if it was taken out, tested resulting in a positive outcome, would they put it back again?" The specialist told me my only option was to take it out... I told him that I appreciated his business but as something had gone into my body naturally, it would go out naturally... so I started to heal myself, first with food, then deep healing with Rebirthing Breathwork, sound healing, emotional healing. I never felt anything else in my whole body, and I never made it back to the specialist office.... Only to advise him I didn't need him and I healed myself.

I started with food, cleaning out the fridge and pantry, buying organic fruit and veggies, juice, water and intermitted fasting, liver cleanses, you name it and I've done it.

Other ways of detoxing were removing many products from our house. Chemicals had to go and instead I shopped at health shops and visited local farmers' markets. Slowly our bodies started to change not just weight dropped off, but our body shape started to change, regenerating all the amazing cells in our bodies, cleansing on a deep cellular level.

During one of my retreats, I met this incredible man Suntara who held a profound Rebirthing Breathwork and Sound healing session. Afterwards, he told me he had only one spot left for his very special Breathwork practitioner course, so in a blink, I joined in with excitement and joy. I experienced many breathwork sessions before, but this was different. He said to me when I entered the room "Life will never be the same" and during the week's intense course, I had such out-of-this-world experiences as I was so ready and open to receive all that was needed to heal me deeply. I sat for eight hours with a fire, gathering wood, keeping the fire going, staring into the fire and just letting go of what no longer served me... well that was a LOT.... Tears rolling down my cheeks, writing journals full of the rollercoaster ride of emotions that flood over me. Whilst in session, I dived so deep I was transcended into many other dimensions and astral travelling into different worlds. He had never experienced someone having such a deep and profound experience which truly change my life. The Breath is the glue between the spirit and the body, it's our anchor to the present.

Now I am also a Rebirthing and Polarity Bodywork practitioner assisting others in this incredible gentle way of breathing to heal and let go of trauma, which is so profound.

I was never felt, heard, seen or understood... I spoke a different "language" that I couldn't explain to others till I completed my Masters of NLP, TimeLine Therapy and Hypnose, making perfect sense and completing the missing piece of my puzzle, which is the fast track path to emotional healing, Mastering your Mindset, changing your words to reflect and express your feelings. Deciding to stop suffering and pain by getting out of your head and into your heart is the hardest journey we all face...

"When the student is ready, the teacher will appear" and many teachers have appeared for me in the past and present, but I love that the student/teacher role works both ways and now I am being the Teacher in other people's lives.

I experienced my Darkest Hours during a weekend of a plant-based medicine journey with an Ayahuasca experience. Even though I lived in Amsterdam where anything is possible, I'm still a naïve girl who has never done any drugs in my life. When I tried some of this plant medicine I didn't feel anything till an extra sip was given. As many journeys are beautiful and have profound results in releasing old baggage, I went the other way and found myself in the Under-world, seeing dark entities and I actually saw so much that I didn't feel safe anymore. We decided to walk away from the scene, following my gut feel, finding our way back home walking bare feet on the asphalt for over 12kms in the dark... this journey is one to be told in another book as it's just an insane ride we were on for days

It let me see my Shadow side, experiencing the Dark Night of my soul, being in different dimensions and seeing Heaven on Earth, I felt the Unconditional Love from and for my husband. It allowed me to let go of my ego and follow my soul purpose in life as a spiritual being living a human life here on Earth. I died, rebirthed and I am alive again.

YES, You truly need to Break Down before You Break Through!

This led me to dive deeper into my soul work, deciding to work with an incredible coach and spiritual healer Tracey and her husband Greg. What intrigued me was the work she does in the 43rd dimension, a way I couldn't really comprehend but had experienced similar during my breathwork sessions and I wanted more of this in my life. But it scared me and left me wondering if it was possible to access this state again... I didn't feel safe doing this work on my own and required guidance to go there. She assisted me to cleanse on a very deep emotional and cellular level, aligning my body, mind and soul. Finding my soul purpose and stepping into my True self allowing myself to share my wisdom, manifest and upgrade to the next level…

I am called a light worker, a healer, and being on my soul journey I was afraid to open up, hiding my gifts until I brought them to the light with her. As messages dropped in I learned to just Trust, trust myself and others and Trust the Process.

As I truly commit to my healing journey, not just rearranging the sh…t to look pretty, my life starts to unravel in a way I never expected. Even in the biggest wildest storm, there is always the calm ocean where I finally listen and honoured my true inner self

I don't need to be fixed as I'm not broken, no need to search for what I've been missing, as I found what I'm looking for, no need to be healed as I heal myself, but it's when I made the decision to stop the suffering and start healing myself and all the seven generations behind and ahead of me, is where I found the true peace within the authentic ME and my high self.

I broke my old habits and patterns, busted through emotional barriers and limiting beliefs, got rid of all the BS stories made up in my head and others told me. I took all my learnings, became fully aware, made decisions easily and effortlessly, and changed my thoughts, words and feelings so I create and manifest, love myself and truly live in the Now. I took full responsibility as when I blamed anyone else for my actions, I saw the three fingers pointed back at me…

I changed my inner landscape to reflect my outer world, as it all starts with me, then creating the ripple effect onto others

I am Perfectly Imperfect, a Work in Progress, living my soul journey in alignment, without ego and from my heart and "It's a Journey without a Destination"

I do not live in that box everyone wants me to be in…

I'm the weird one,

I've never fitted in the box…. And I never will 🖤…

And that's ok and so it is!

ABOUT NICOLETTE WIJERS

Nicolette Wijers is the founder of Simply The Best Life. She is the Emotional Alchemist who assists stressed and overworked women to Awaken to their soul purpose, find their authentic selves and transform to live life to their fullest potential in love, joy and happiness.

Originally from The Netherlands, Nicolette started her career in the hospitality industry working extremely long hours, never had time to spend with her friends and family, missing out on all the fun things in life, as she worked from the bottom and all the way up just in search of her ultimate top job in luxury hotels and resorts.

Her desire to free herself from being stuck and stressed, her drive to find the Awakened Feminine within her, lead her to her "Journey without a Destination" of consistent growth, going within where she creates her Soul purpose.

Now she empowers her clients to transmute emotional suffering, unhealthy patterns and habits by releasing the limited beliefs, blocks and programming that stop them from fully embracing a soul-aligned abundant life.

After travelling the world with her husband, she now lives in Australia.

Website: *www.nicolettewijers.com*
Email: *nicolette.wijers@gmail.com*
Facebook: *www.facebook.com/TheNicoletteWijers*
LinkedIn: *www.linkedin.com/in/nicolette-wijers-groenendijk*

2 2

TEENA RYAN

Elizabeth Gilbert says "we are all walking repositories of buried treasure...the hunt to uncover those jewels—that's creative living. The courage to go on the hunt in the first place, that's what separates a mundane existence from a more enchanted one."

We each come to this life with a purpose, a "mission" **so to speak.** Some are fortunate enough to discover theirs early in life, and for others, it takes a series of unfortunate events designed by our souls to uncover our own buried treasure.

It has taken a culmination of all my life events for me to uncover my buried treasure and to discover my true purpose and how I discovered the power in following my divinely given intuitive abilities instead of relying solely on logic, analysis and reason.

I was a closet control freak. I didn't feel free enough to truly be all that I was designed to be; I wore a carefully constructed mask. It hid a painful secret: my innocence was robbed by my maternal grandfather when I was five.

It changed a once happy, intuitively guided little girl who loved gymnastics and playing with Barbie dolls with her cousins, to a little girl who craved control.

I desperately needed to know what was coming next, to carefully construct every situation to be guaranteed an outcome and ensure that I felt safe and secure.

I no longer trusted my intuitive abilities, they had abandoned me in my time of need, like a discarded puppy on the side of the road.

My mother read me a poem consistently throughout my childhood:

> *There was a little girl,*
> *Who had a little curl,*
> *Right in the middle of her forehead.*
> *When she was good,*
> *She was very, very good,*
> *But when she was bad, she was horrid.*
> *But when she was bad, she was horrid.*

Can you imagine the impact that had on me?

The thought of being horrid and not being loved by my parents was so scary to me so I became the "yes" girl.

So, I followed the traditional success model—the "Good Girl Playbook"

I got a good education and was the first in my family to obtain tertiary qualifications.

At nineteen, I met a charming, charismatic man at work, one date led to another and another until we moved in together.

I worked hard, we got engaged, we bought a house and got married in front of 110 of our closest family and friends.

We settled down, renovated our home, and decided to start a family.

I had a burning desire to be a mother, an inner knowing that it was part of my life's purpose; however, I didn't realise it would take five years and nine rounds of IVF treatments to finally become a mother. The treatments were invasive, took the beauty and romance out of creating a child, and left you feeling like a battery caged hen. Being injected with hormones, prodded, and poked, having to let go of your modesty to produce your heart's desire, often resulted in heart breaking disappointment. I was one of the "lucky ones," though I didn't see it that way at the time—seven rounds of treatment including four egg retrievals to fall pregnant with my first miracle, Thomas and a further two rounds, three years later for my second miracle, Darcy to make his long-awaited entrance.

After my second son and I came home from hospital, the wheels began to fall off my marriage. My husband did not cope well with our second son coming into the world and said things that a new mother doesn't ever want to hear. I experienced an emotional death at that moment. My heart had been irreparably broken but I had made a commitment, I made vows to this man:

> *For better or worse*
> *For richer or poorer*
> *In sickness and in health*
> *Until death do us part*

How much worse did it have to get?

How much more was I willing to take?

I relied solely on my intellect to make decisions throughout my life —my inner control freak was most certainly in the driver's seat.

The thought of walking away from my marriage and breaking up our family seemed so inconceivable at the time. So, I did the good girl thing: I sucked up my own unhappiness, concentrated on the health and happiness of my boys and slowly began to shut off my heart. I became a _very_ good actress. I played the role of a dutiful wife and mother, business owner and eldest sister.

I was so envious of my friends who seemed ridiculously happy in their lives and marriages, who seemed to have it all, but appearances are deceiving. My assumption was their relationships were ideal. I was jealous of something I felt was unattainable for me. I kept searching for something that would bring me happiness, buying vintage collectables, antique jewellery, anything to fill the gaping hole that was my heart and soul.

Five years later, a very good friend asked me one of the most profound questions I had ever heard.

"Who are you without your labels—wife, mother, sister, daughter, business owner, friend?"

It was a question I had no answer for. I had placed all my value in those labels and in my relationship with my husband.

Who am I? Now that was the $50 million question!

The same good friend started a women's circle where I was first introduced to meditation. Meditation was my gateway to my awakening. I began to slowly reconnect with my intuitive abilities, felt calmer when dealing with my boys, and began to not sweat the small stuff.

My intuition had sent subtle messages, hints and tips and it wasn't until my intuition started behaving like a child in the supermarket having a tantrum, that I began to listen. The sleepless nights, the vivid dreams showing a radically different version of my life and a sick feeling in the pit of my stomach, were some of the not-so-subtle indicators that the direction of my life was about to change.

I slowly began to trust the messages that I was receiving, and the strange thing was, the more time I spent working out who I was, on my journey of self-discovery, the more desperate my husband became to keep me exactly where I was.

He constantly asked, "where has the girl that I met gone to?"

Well, the answer was I wasn't THAT girl anymore. I had traversed marriage, motherhood, business ownership, challenging relationships and life in general which meant I wasn't the girl he met in the beginning, anymore. I was discovering I was more than the labels I had placed, and others had placed on me.

I paid attention to the interactions between my friends and their partners and how they treated each other. Love, honesty, open communication, happiness…It did not reflect what was happening in my home. I was constantly asking for support raising our boys, I desperately wanted my husband to share in the day-to-day of parenthood, but his sole focus was the business and making money.

His behaviour, actions, and how he chose to speak to me caused me to turn inwards. To rely solely on myself for emotional support, love and kindness. I was desperately lonely whilst in my marriage, feeling like a single parent and it wasn't what I wanted or needed. I had emotionally checked out of my marriage, I became a hollowed-out shell who pretended that her life was perfect, when it absolutely wasn't.

The day after my first son turned twelve, I finally reached my shit tolerance level. I was exhausted emotionally, physically, mentally, and spiritually from needing to be constantly in battle-ready mode—running on adrenaline and having nothing left to give.

The words "I'm done" finally came from the depths of my soul. It was my intuitive voice that spoke the day I asked for a divorce.

I'M DONE, I'M DONE, I'M DONE
With not knowing who I truly am
With being "The good girl"
With being predictable
With being his verbal punching bag
With being scared for my boys and myself
With being afraid of what my future would look like
With other people telling me how to live my life
With doing things that didn't excite me
With constantly putting other people first
With holding back
With worrying about other people's opinions on how I mother, how I love, how I move, how I live, how I serve my community
With allowing my past to rule my present and my future
With the shoulds and the have-to's
With being lonely in a marriage and staying together for the sake of appearances
With trying to make my marriage work

The shock that registered on his face was surprising because I truly thought he felt as miserable as I did but just wasn't courageous enough to say so. The bigger surprise came later from my family and friends, which was a harder pill to swallow.

I was no longer wearing the labels (dutiful, long-suffering wife, pushover, good girl, "yes woman") that people could easily identify with. I was wearing ones that they had no experience in dealing with.

I wasn't the daughter that rang to complain about my marriage and what I thought was missing and how I wished it was different.

I was now a single mother, on the road to being a divorcee, and a woman discovering who she was underneath it all. A woman who wore a genuine smile more often, who was happier even though she was grieving the loss of her marriage.

Every challenge, every upheaval, every argument, every interaction was preparing me for what my soul desired; the ability to make choices that served and suited me, discovering who I truly was.

I had a burning desire to shed the conditioning and trauma that held me back from stepping into my life's purpose. My purpose wasn't crystal clear and as frustrating as it was, I knew I was meant for something more.

A friend recently said it's not the darkness within us that we fear, but it's actually our light.

We are fearful of shining brightly, loving ourselves like the priceless gems we are, and sharing our magic, and our medicine. We don't want to lose ourselves, our comfortable lives, and the love and support of those around us. It's scary to step away from everything you've known in favour of a new, never-trodden path that has no guarantees of success.

I had no doubt that walking that path was necessary to ensure I was being the best version of myself and showing my boys what was possible when you had faith that what you were doing was right for all concerned.

I knew that I had to make the change in order to be the best mum I could be to my boys.

Our situation had to change in order to ensure that we all had the best possible environment in which we could be our best possible versions.

With the death of my marriage and living arrangements came my rebirth.

With that rebirth came a new mantra that my intuition began to chant:

I'm ready

I'm ready

I'm ready

I'm ready to allow my intuition to come out of the shadows and begin flexing her muscles again. I wasn't ready to give her the driver's seat, but I was more willing to listen to the directions she was offering.

I'm ready to peel back the layers of conditioning and habitual patterns and to flush out my ugly with a fire hose. I'm ready to begin healing from the experiences of my childhood, to deal with the trauma and to seek a new way of being. I'm ready to be fully immersed, to be all in on my personal growth

I'm ready to discover who I am and try some new labels on for size —Single Mum, Independent Woman, Rule Breaker, Permission Giver, Conscious Communicator, Intuitively Guided Woman

I'm ready to embrace what this season of my life will look like, to accept the wild abundance that is waiting for me and to uncover what I truly desire.

I'm ready to live again.

Living on my own for the first time was disconcerting. Having been a 24/7 parent catering to my children's every need, to having one week to myself, I felt completely lost.

What was I meant to do with my time? Work only filled so much time, the silence was deafening and completely foreign to me.

I walked kilometres upon kilometres at the beach with my dog, I discovered a love of yoga, and I started my own jewellery business.

I discovered that I loved a glass of scotch at the end of the day and ate vegetarian food to my heart's content.

I spent hours journaling, working through my grief, my trauma, my heart's desire for my new life and the feeling that I had failed my kids.

I did discover it was easier to be lonely and alone than lonely and in a relationship. Explaining to my boys why we could no longer be a family was a tough conversation and that's putting it mildly. The one promise I did make to them was that I would be completely honest.

Being a single mum was an eye-opening experience.

How you are viewed by other parents, how other women see you, and how quickly I was expected to find another relationship. I desired to have a relationship with myself for the first time in forever, to fall in love with the woman I was becoming.

I wasn't ready or willing to share my space with another human being. The thought of dating was scary, to say the least. Dating apps held no appeal after the disaster stories I had heard.

It took eighteen months to feel ready to dip my toe into that pool.

My intuition was leading the charge. I met some interesting humans and the man I've chosen to share my life with.

Six years on, the lens through which I view my life is radically different, and I love the concept of living creatively.

I found true, mind-blowing, out-of-this-world love, something that I never expected or dreamed was possible.

To have a true partner in life and love and a man I can experience emotional, intellectual, spiritual, experiential, and physical intimacy with is a complete 180 to the life I use to live.

I have surrendered and allowed my intuition to lead. I'm no longer obsessed with being in the driver's seat controlling every single aspect of my life because I've discovered it's no way to live.

I am extremely intentional with my words, my actions, how I express myself and I show up unapologetically and "unashamedly me."

I love everything about my life, and I've met some of the most amazing humans who have enhanced my life in ways that I never dreamed would be possible.

I radically lead myself, and I own when I make mistakes and embrace the needed course corrections.

I embrace each season of my life and all the joy, love, happiness and fun that it brings

I open my arms to the wild abundance that the universe will deliver to me, as I play in the realm of infinite possibilities.

I allow myself to feel all my emotions, good, bad or indifferent. I live from a space of joy and pleasure, and I give others wild permission to do the same. I've learnt to give myself all the love and support that I readily give to others

I share my magic, my wisdom, and my knowledge so that I may act as a lighthouse for others.

I love watching my boys learn how to radically lead themselves, to follow their own destinies and honour their own intuitive gifts. They are kind, emotionally intelligent, decent young men who have had the opportunity to see their mother become the best version of herself.

I have realised that I don't have to have all the answers and to allow life to unfold as it's designed to.

I live a peaceful, harmonious life of my own design, I no longer have to be battle-ready each and every day though living with teenagers does test your ability to respond rather than react!

For every stage in life, there is a period of death and rebirth

The shedding of old ways, thoughts, ideas, beliefs, feelings, patterns, and labels as you begin to embody new knowledge, values, and concepts and move closer to who you truly are.

The question is are you brave enough to become an archaeologist in your own life?

Are you courageous enough to go on the hunt for your own buried treasure, to step bravely into the unknown, to look fear in the eye, allow your intuitive voice to be an active contributor and live a life filled with possibility and passion?

Don't hide your beauty!

Expose your facets to the light, shine like the bright brilliant gems that you are and live the most audacious life possible!

ABOUT TEENA RYAN

Teena specializes in turning energy-sapping relationships into juicy, joyful experiences that light you up and fill your cup so you can live your most audacious life.

Teena's eight-step process helps...

...you to discover a harmonious balance between your masculine and feminine traits. If the delicate dance between the two is not in alignment, it often feels forced leaving you feeling extremely dissatisfied. Teena guides you to choreograph a new routine to ensure the movement between the two is seamless.

...to reframe your most pressing challenges into opportunities for growth and expansion, helping you to regain that "loving feeling" for yourself and for your life.

...to guide you back to your inner knowing, to trust your intuitive guidance rather than operating from the neck up and acting like Mr. Potato Head.

> **Website:** *www.dharmasandco.com.au*
> **LinkedIn:** *www.linkedin.com/in/teena-ryan-07022a89/*
> **Facebook:** *www.facebook.com/dharmasnco*
> **Instagram:** *www.instagram.com/dharmasnco*

ABOUT AMA PUBLISHING

AMA Publishing is an international, award winning publishing company that champions the stories of entrepreneurs who are trailblazers, innovators, and instigators.

Forbes has said that, *"AMA Publishing is helping women reshape the future of publishing."*

We would love to help you tell your story. We have helped thousands of people become international, bestselling authors through our courses, multi-author books, and as solo authors.

Your story, it's ready to be told.

Website: *www.amapublishing.co*